"When choosing a spouse, learning to ask the right questions is essential to making a wise choice—and that's exactly what Kimberly Beair helps readers do in *First Comes Love, Then What?*"

—Gary Thomas

"In this age when the message of movies, songs, and novels is that intense romance and passion are the foundation of lasting marriages, Christian therapist Kim Beair brings a solid, practical approach to help you determine whether your love relationship is based on love versus lust, or trust versus fantasy. *First Comes Love, Then What?* is an interactive book designed to deepen your understanding of yourself, your future mate, and most importantly, your relationship with God. This book crosses generations. Buy it if you are engaged or contemplating marriage, or buy it for someone close to you who is in a seriously committed relationship. I hope that Bible study groups across this country will use this book to guide people to lasting relationships so that Christians are once again known for their passion for Christ and passion for marriage and family."

—Earl R. Henslin Psy.D., B.C.E.T.S.

MFT 14693

Board Certified Expert in Traumatic Stress

Diplomate in the American Academy of Experts in Traumatic Stress

first comes love, then what?

first comes love,
then
what?
what

Kimberly Beair, MS LPC

Tyndale House Publishers, Inc., Carol Stream, Illinois

First Comes Love, Then What?
Copyright © 2008 by Kimberly Beair
All rights reserved. International copyright secured.

A Focus on the Family book published by
Tyndale House Publishers, Inc., Carol Stream, Illinois 60188

Focus on the Family and the accompanying logo and design are federally registered trademarks of Focus on the Family, Colorado Springs, CO 80995.

TYNDALE and Tyndale's quill logo are registered trademarks of Tyndale House Publishers, Inc.

All Scripture quotations, unless otherwise indicated, are taken from the *Holy Bible, New International Version®*. NIV®. Copyright © 1973, 1978, 1984 by International Bible Society. Used by permission of Zondervan Publishing House. All rights reserved.

Scripture quotations marked (ESV) are taken from *The Holy Bible, English Standard Version,* copyright © 2001 by Crossway Bibles, a division of Good News Publishers. Used by permission. All rights reserved.

The majority of case examples presented in this book are fictional composites based on the author's clinical experience with hundreds of clients through the years. Any resemblance between these fictional characters and actual persons is coincidental. When clients' actual stories have been used, people's names and certain details of their stories have been changed to protect the privacy of the individuals involved.

Editors: Mary Ann Jeffreys, Liz Duckworth
Cover design: Jennifer Ghionzoli
Cover photograph by Veer. All rights reserved.

Library of Congress Cataloging-in-Publication Data
Beair, Kimberly, 1962-
  First comes love, then what? : challenging your assumptions on dating,
love, and marriage / Kimberly Beair.
    p. cm.
  "A Focus on the Family book."
  ISBN-13: 978-1-58997-448-7
  ISBN-10: 1-58997-448-4
  1. Marriage—Religious aspects—Christianity. 2. Love—Religious aspects—Christianity.
3. Dating (Social customs)—Religious aspects—Christianity. I. Title.
  BV835.B355 2008
  241'.6765—dc22
                                        2007036577

Printed in the United States of America
1 2 3 4 5 6 7 8 9 / 13 12 11 10 09 08

This book is dedicated to God and the people I love:

Brian, for 25 amazing years of letting me be me; that is love.

Kara, my beautiful daughter and partner;
none of my projects would exist without you.

Brian Lee, you are the bravest person I know;
your courage inspires me.

Mom and Dad, my models of wisdom and discernment.

Todd and Kurt, brothers like no other;
your friendships are more precious than gold.

Contents

Introduction

What happens when you contemplate being in a romantic relationship? Do you get a funny feeling in the pit of your stomach as you daydream about that *someone* you are certain is out there? When you think about spending your life with one person, do you feel excitement, confusion, fear—or possibly all three? Do you think about your past relationships and wonder if there *is* a spouse in your future?

No matter which of these thoughts and feelings the words "romantic relationship" evoke, this is the book for you.

It's no secret that the vast majority of Americans choose to marry. Sadly, however, society today is plagued by more abusive, unhappy, and failed marriages than ever before. Every generation wants desperately to break the cycle of serious marital problems and divorce, but most people don't know where to begin. Let your study of this book be a first step in launching healthy new habits for the sake of your future *successful* relationships.

First, I need to burst a bubble of mythology that says good marriages "just happen." Not true. All relationships are complicated, and maintaining a successful one requires a great deal of work on the part of both individuals involved. This remains true for every stage of the relationship.

This book is truly for anyone interested in pursuing a positive marital relationship. Perhaps you have had your share of interesting relationships, and you believe they served a purpose (though you may not be *exactly* certain what that purpose was). Maybe you've also watched some of your nearest and dearest friends get themselves into messy relationships. You might be worried that you'll find yourself in the same situation. Be assured, you can find someone with whom you can enjoy a happy and healthy life, but finding the right life mate will not happen through luck or chance.

View this book as a wise friend in your search for a healthy relationship. As you read, you will obtain information vital to having a happy and long-lasting marriage. Having this information prior to beginning a relationship puts you way ahead of the game. As you work through the material at the end of each chapter, you'll be able to evaluate and apply these key concepts in your own life. Employing these principles during your dating years and later married life should greatly improve your relationships and potentially save you (and others) pain, disappointment, and perhaps some hefty legal and therapy fees.

If you are currently involved in a serious relationship, this book will help you determine if you should continue moving forward. If you've been in relationships that have failed, perhaps you need to reevaluate your strategies. Some of your past experiences may have led you to question whether Mr. or Ms. Right is even out there. Make it a goal to identify where you've gone wrong in the past so you can make wise choices for your upcoming dating relationships. Have confidence that you can start anew and develop a positive, meaningful, and lasting relationship for the future.

In the following chapters, you will discover what motivates people in relationships—consciously, subconsciously, and unconsciously. You will be guided to take a closer look at yourself. You can get started right now by considering the following questions:

- Do you consciously know what type of person you hope to share your life with?
- Do you know which values are most important in your life?
- Do you know your personality type?
- Do you know which personality types are most compatible with yours?
- Do you know as much about yourself as you think?
- Do you know as much about yourself as you want to know?

I hope you will always be willing to learn more about who you are, what makes you tick, and where you are going in life. This book will teach you a lot about yourself! Why is that important? Because you can't find a compatible mate or work on your current relationship without first knowing who *you* are. Another major element of successful relationships involves how you interact with other people, and this will be examined in detail as well. Just remember, most people make the mistake of thinking their relationship issues are unique, but in reality, they are not. Take comfort in the fact that you are not alone.

This book was written with *you* in mind and is intended to help you be miles ahead when you ultimately walk down the aisle. A strong foundation is the basis of a successful marriage, and this book will help you build it.

One great way to understand how various factors each play a role in relationships and why many people pair up with partners who are not good matches is to examine a variety of real relationships. In each highlighted relationship in this book, we will study individuals and learn from their mistakes as well as their good choices. Note how the unhealthy decisions made by some and the healthy decisions made by others impacted their relationships in both the short term and long term.

To make the most of your experience with this book, pay particular attention to the Reality Check at the end of each chapter. This checkpoint section was designed to help you reflect on each chapter's content and relate it to your own personal dating relationships. If you have a dating partner, have him or her read the book and answer the questions as well. This will be helpful, because couples often fail to share their thoughts as well as future expectations about a long-term relationship.

As you compare answers with your partner, don't focus on whether your answers are alike or different. Focus instead on healthy, nonjudgmental conversation, and really get to know each other while building healthy communication skills. With the right attitude, you will grow in knowledge about yourself, your partner, and the relationship as a whole.

Check out the "words of wisdom" quotes throughout each chapter, evaluate them, and ask yourself how you respond to them.

Compare your experiences with our group of two hundred singles surveyed for the Singles Say… sections.

Remember that no matter who you are or where you come from, having a successful relationship is no easy feat. It takes a well-stocked toolbox, two dedicated and committed partners, and lots of hard, yet rewarding, work. By absorbing the information here, you are putting one more tool in your toolbox. You will begin to understand and debunk relationship myths perpetuated by society and unlock secrets to success so your job becomes a little easier. You will learn a lot about yourself, your friends, and your relatives, and you'll hopefully improve the way you approach this adventure of a lifetime.

(1)

Challenging Your Assumptions

How many of us take the time to develop a logical approach to love and marriage? All too often we rush in and base our decisions on the prevailing wisdom. Often the assumptions we make—assumptions based on what we've learned from friends, family, experience, and every form of media—are faulty to begin with. Every decision flowing from a wrong assumption will be distorted.

You may be able to come up with your personal list of false assumptions, but here are five common misconceptions we can look at as we begin *First Comes Love, Then What?*

FALSE ASSUMPTION #1:
THERE IS ONE PERFECT SOUL MATE FOR EACH PERSON

Let's start off with the soul-mate question since it's one that generates debate, discussion, and controversy among a large number of young men and women.

Jessica, a pastor in the Midwest, tells the story of finding her "soul mate." At a young age, she found Mr. Right, who also happened to be a pastor. They seemed "destined to be together" prior to the marriage, but shortly after they said "I do," her pastor husband became abusive. For years, she said, they lived the lie of the perfect family while behind closed doors their marriage was a shambles, and they were both distanced from God.

When Jessica got married, she still believed there was one "right person" for her. When the marriage failed, she said, "I married the wrong man. This was not the man God had planned for me." She credited her mistake to youth, lack of wisdom, discernment, judgment, and plain ignoring the warning signs all around her. She had told herself he was her soul mate and moved forward without doing her homework (the things this book suggests).

> "Happiness is not a reward—it is a consequence. Suffering is not a punishment—it is a result."
> ROBERT GREEN INGERSOLL

Jessica now admits that if she had done her homework, perhaps she and her husband could have worked out some healthy boundaries and expectations before they wed, potentially alleviating the problems they encountered.

Jessica is learning from her mistakes. She no longer believes that God has "one right person" for her—that was just her romanticized ideal. She also says, "Look at it this way—we meet many friends in life, and if we work on those relationships, they grow, mature, and last over time. So doesn't it stand to reason we could literally choose just about anyone who is compatible, put time and energy into the relationship, and find a spouse who feels like a soul mate?"

Ask a number of teenagers or young adults what they think about the concept of a soul mate, and you will likely find a high number of them believe in predestined love. Ask people over 50, and you will find far fewer who believe in the concept 100 percent. Instead they believe wise choices and hard work have everything to do with relationship success.

Harry and Fern have been married 50 years and believe they are soul mates, but their definition of that term has changed over time. They tell stories about having been on the brink of divorce years earlier, with conflict during their first 20 years. This couple took advantage of counseling and resources before they were commonplace and now state, "A good marriage is a lot of hard work."

Fern believes couples buying into the soul-mate concept use it as an excuse to neither do their homework on the front end nor tend to the relationship once they marry—a mistake she and Harry made for years. She believes couples give way to intense loving feelings that fade over time and leave relationships in shambles. She tells of asking herself how things could go so wrong if she and Harry were truly meant for each other. Now she thinks of the term *soul mate* differently. She still believes she and Harry were destined to be together but admits they could have easily broken up and moved on in their lives separately. Today, when she uses the term *soul mate*, she thinks of the energy, time, and hard work they put into their relationship to turn lemons into lemonade.

Harry says, "Just because people think they were meant to be together doesn't mean it will last!"

There's good news about letting go of the soul-mate theory. You do have the freedom to choose your life mate from among lots of candidates. You also have the potential to make the right marriage for you happen—along with the agreement of the man or woman you select, of course.

Falling in love can be both frightening and exhilarating at the same time. In the swirl of the strong feelings falling in love generates, many people wonder how to *know* they have found their marriage partner, and what a great marriage with that person will look and feel like. While some people, and perhaps you too, still hold to the "one person out there waiting for me" theory, remember that making a marriage takes two people using their free will to come to the same conclusion. Even if you think God has predestined you to be together, each of you still has free will to accept or reject the other's thoughts, feelings, and expectations.

Free will is a gift of God. We read in the Bible about King Solomon, who was blessed and ordained to be a great king. He also asked God for wisdom, and this request seemed pleasing to God. If God ordained and predestined Solomon to be a great king, why would he need to ask God for wisdom? Wouldn't it stand to reason that God would just wave His omnipotent hand and supply everything Solomon would need to be great? We see in Solomon's story (told in 1 Kings 4–5; 11) examples of great wisdom but also of great mistakes. It is clear he loved women and blatantly went against God's plan by allowing pagan women to permeate his life and home, to his detriment.

God has great things in store for all of us, but He will never force us to obey. Remember that in the Garden of Eden Adam and Eve ate from the tree in the center of the garden. They were told not to, but the tree wasn't fenced off. It was their decision whether to obey God and have the good life designed for them. Unfortunately, they became deceived and gave up the freedom and innocence intended for the human race.

Speaking of Adam and Eve, their story is the only one in the Bible where you will find a woman specifically created for her man. Perhaps the creation story of man and woman prompts the idea there is a special mate intended for each person. I personally would love to buy into this idea and believe there is one right person for everyone destined to be married. What counters that concept, however, is the rest of the Bible, which gives detailed information on the kinds of people we are to be wary of, the kinds of behaviors that kill and thrill in relationships, and most of all, it admonishes us to use wisdom and discernment in decisions of all kinds.

Whether or not there is one person chosen for you, will you do what *you* need to do on the front end to find that right person, then ensure you nurture yourself, your partner, and the relationship? Or do you just want to wait for the one you believe has been predestined, imagine him or her falling into your lap, and then do nothing to make this special relationship grow and mature into something wonderful?

If there is no "one person" out there, should you just look around for someone, anyone, using a wish list of characteristics you find appealing? (Do the exercise under Write It Down at the end of the chapter to compile your wish list.) If you follow this method, remember you have the power to

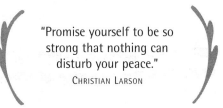

"Promise yourself to be so strong that nothing can disturb your peace."
CHRISTIAN LARSON

choose, so choose well. If the number of available partners with most or all your wish-list characteristics seems slim, should you throw out your wish list? Absolutely not. Your historical pattern might have been to delete certain items from the wish list because a potential date was having difficulty meeting that criteria. You may have ended up saying to yourself, *This guy is halfway decent, so why shouldn't I form a long-term relationship with him?* Make no mistake: in this situation, your prescription is to stick to your list. Of course, you may feel that sticking to the list might cause it to take longer to find a mate than compromising right now.

If you have compromised in the past, where has it taken you? Probably not to your desired destination of "happily ever after." Commit to give the next search some time, be patient, and wait for the mate who fits your list. With sharper vision, skills, and dedication, you might discover that finding your mate takes less time than you thought it would, and you won't have to compromise your relationship, yourself, or your future.

What happens if you marry the "wrong mate"? All hope is not lost. As with any of our best-laid plans, we can all be deceived or overlook something, either intentionally or unintentionally. Whatever the case, when we have not chosen as wisely as possible, we can still hope to make a difficult relationship work, especially if we have already eliminated as many roadblocks as we could from the beginning. It still takes work on the part of *both* people in the relationship, but it is possible to be successful.

In actuality, millions of people do find their true life mates and enjoy great lives together. Yet history will often show how these people took the time and effort to choose wisely, then worked the kinks out together as problems came along. So the definition of the "right" or "wrong" person is only as good as the work put in ahead of time and throughout the duration of the relationship.

Even problematic relationships can be worked out between two people with healthy attitudes and the goal of relationship success. Ultimately, the popular myth of a soul mate is just that—a myth.

FALSE ASSUMPTION #2:
YOUR LIFE MATE COMPLETES WHO YOU ARE

Your life is a journey with an intended purpose bigger than any relationship. Do you put your life in Park once you're in a relationship? Many people go through life thinking that finding the perfect mate is their ultimate destination. Such a person finds the love of her life and then quits growing. Even if she goes to work or starts a family, she really expects the relationship to create all her happiness. Once people like this have been "parked" there for a while, the scenery becomes boring, especially when the initial feelings of burning love begin to fade. These people are left with disappointment, wondering, "Is that all there is?"

If you were taking a road-trip vacation, you would plan the trip, see lots of sights along the way, spend a few days at the Grand Canyon, have all the fun you could, then return home. Parking in a relationship is like heading out on that trip, but upon getting to the

Grand Canyon, you park the car at one of the overlook sites and keep gazing at the one view. After a while, you begin to get bored with the beautiful view and regret not doing all the other things you had planned for your journey.

In a similar way, your *life* is a journey, and relationships should flow with you in that journey, not keep you from God's bigger purpose for your life.

The people you allow to join your journey need to fit into your purpose and complement it. Don't park in a relationship thinking *that* is your ulti-

> "My best friend is the one who brings out the best in me."
> HENRY FORD

mate purpose. Decide on your purpose in life and expect your relationships to fit in to it. When you do that, you will likely discover you don't make many of the mistakes you made in previous relationships. In turn, you will be happier and more balanced in every area of your life, including your relationships—a true win/win situation.

Many of you are asking, "How do I know what my purpose is?" This is not a mystical question involving great soul searching. God has created you with unique and special gifts. He knows just who you will be and what purposes He has for you. Read Psalm 139:1-16. Trust that the right path is laid out before you, and ask God to direct your steps. You may not feel that you can see where the path ends, but sometimes the important thing is staying on the right path, and you will get where you are supposed to be.

Your purpose in life doesn't even have to be anything out of the ordinary. Check out the woman described in Proverbs 31:10-31. She's described as a wife of noble character who sews, cooks, farms, buys and sells, cares for the poor, works out at the gym (see verse 17), and generally manages her household and her family.

The Scriptures are stocked with people of great and mighty faith and power, yet in reading about the wife of noble character, we see that she is *only* (ha!) *a working mom.* These verses basically describe many hardworking women (and men) then and now. Most people don't see the daily grind as anything wonderful or amazing, but these verses remind us about the purpose and value of the regular activities of daily life lived with integrity.

So what is the right path for you?

- Toni is a 26-year-old single female working full time and attending law school at night. For the moment, she needs to focus on being the best student and employee she can be, while keeping herself healthy with exercise and good nutrition so she can combat stress and illness.
- Duane is a 32-year-old single dad with two active boys. He works full time, gets the boys to all their activities, and volunteers at the church four hours each week to help with their computer issues.
- Brent is a 20-year-old full-time college student attempting to graduate and go into the air force.
- Shel is a 37-year-old single mother recuperating from a car accident and is off work until she is healed. While at home, she is taking a few online classes to increase her skills and make good use of her time.
- Shanna is a 28-year-old single female working every day. She has decided to work out four times each week and take a cooking class.

Toni, Duane, Brent, Shel, and Shanna are all dating; they just make sure their dates don't take time away from their present priorities. And those priorities are different for each person depending on his or her goals and responsibilities. What are your priorities today?

Your priorities are often determined by your life's purpose, though it might seem as if they are actually driven by your immediate "to do" list. Have you taken the time to consider why you were put on this earth? Does God have a specific role for you to play or a plan for you to fulfill? Or have you always just done the next thing on your list, without really wondering about the bigger picture of your life's plan?

The process of fulfilling your purpose does not require you to become the next Oprah Winfrey or Bill Gates. In the case of the people described on the previous page, the main purpose for each is to stay on track with current responsibili-

"You will eat the fruit of your labor."
PSALM 128:2

ties and not be distracted by making dating relationships the first priority. In some cases, the people described are dealing with unexpected curves in life's road or added responsibilities or activities. The important thing is that we must take care of our priorities first, including our minds, bodies, spirits, souls, and dependent family members. Outside relationships should follow naturally.

Discovering how to be the best possible "you" will result in wonderful, healthy relationships coming into your life, rather than people who would attempt to drain you. Be a healthy, whole person first, and then add a great relationship on top.

"You complete me" is one of the most popular, romanticized movie lines of our time, as well as one of the most damaging. One person "completing" another implies a person was not "whole" prior to a relationship. We were not created missing anything for the good of our lives, and we have the capability to be complete while standing alone, outside of a romantic relationship. "You complement me" doesn't roll off the tongue or inspire romance as easily, but it is a more healthy way of looking at relationships. Actually, the more a person develops his or her own life, the more respect, interest, and romance can be brought into a couple's relationship.

FALSE ASSUMPTION #3: LOVE CONQUERS ALL

Divorce rates are staggering, and many divorced people ultimately remarry and divorce again. The people who stay in unhappy marriages do so for a variety of reasons: children, money, spiritual beliefs, reputation, career advancement, and so on. As you can imagine, unhappy marriages make for unhappy families, which can lead to more dysfunction over time. Yet most of these troubled marriages started out well, with a couple believing they could endure difficulties because they began with true love.

The belief that love conquers all is a faulty assumption. Love may start out as the foundation of the relationship, just as the Grand Canyon was once a flat piece of hard rock divided by the Colorado River. Despite the rock's solid makeup, erosion over time created huge cracks, crevices, and craters. In the same way, love can be eroded by life's circumstances, creating a "canyon" that seems impossible to cross.

One problem with believing that love conquers all is that there are so many different definitions of love. Some people define love as a feeling, but feelings are fickle, often changing with the latest mood, and they cannot be relied upon as consistent gauges for sound decision making. This is especially true for those people who have never learned how to control their feelings. Generally, people who define love as a feeling are less likely to understand the need to stop, calm down, and reevaluate a situation when their feelings are more stable. If this sounds like you, you may be unaware that you actually have power over your feelings and that they can be tempered with practice.

Others have a more in-depth and reality-based understanding of love that includes patience, kindness, selflessness, consistent boundary setting, commitment, and so on. They might define love as it is described in this passage from the Bible:

Love is patient, love is kind. It does not envy, it does not boast, it is not proud. It is not rude, it is not self-seeking, it is not easily angered, it keeps no record of wrongs. Love does not delight in evil but rejoices with the truth. It always protects, always trusts, always hopes, always perseveres. Love never fails. (1 Corinthians 13:4-8)

While some people believe that commitment, stability, and doing all the right things can conquer a problem, they may ignore feelings altogether. Unfortunately, "doing the right thing" and loving the other person will not always change the thoughts and feelings of the other person within the relationship. In fact, you and your partner may experience the relationship in completely different ways. Unexplored differences between two people can lead to feelings of hurt and confusion. As a result, relationships may break up, regardless of how often a partner practices "doing the right thing." Love doesn't always conquer the differences between two people.

FALSE ASSUMPTION #4:
SHORTCUTS WORK (JUST LOOK AT REALITY TV)

Reality dating shows seem to imply that all you need is a nice pool of choices and a little time to spend together, and you'll find the love of your life. They demonstrate the shortcut method to choosing a mate for life. These shows aren't too different from the concept of "speed dating" where prospective daters get three minutes to interrogate each other before deciding if they want to go further. Decisions are made on the most superficial aspects—appearance especially.

Too often people neglect to consider all aspects of their lives, including family and friend relationships, career goals, worldview differences, and other factors that influence a long-lasting relationship. Relationships move so quickly these days that couples neglect important considerations for a successful marriage. Or they don't foresee problems that can arise from longer-term relationships and therefore can't effectively resolve them. Frankly, some couples put more thought into what kind of car they want to buy than which person they ought to marry.

Unfortunately, we *all* have faulty and unhealthy beliefs about marriage influenced by our own romanticized thoughts, the media, well-meaning friends, and even our own family systems. Young people spend years training for certain careers, but when it comes to finding a mate, they receive either no training at all or misguided training. Some people make unwise choices because they are insecure—and guess what? Their insecurity only worsens.

> "By wisdom a house is built, and through understanding it is established; through knowledge its rooms are filled with rare and beautiful treasures."
> PROVERBS 24:3-4

Remember, when you're seeking a long-term relationship, your faulty beliefs will cause you to go for the shortcut 100 percent of the time. Begin identifying your shortcut approaches to relationships today, and purposely choose to take the long-range, tried-and-true way in these areas. Slow down and think clearly in order to increase your happiness and relationship success.

FALSE ASSUMPTION #5:
THE LAWS OF ATTRACTION DON'T APPLY TO YOU

Just as salt brings out the flavor of food, relationships should bring out the best in each partner. Do your relationships enhance your strengths, or do they totally smother you? Maybe your relationships don't smother you, but they contribute to bringing out your most negative qualities. If your relationships do not enhance your strengths while balancing out your weaknesses, examine why you continue selecting partners who don't complement you.

You cannot fault your dates for this problem. After all, *you* chose to allow the other person into your life. What's going on here? The laws of attraction are very likely in play.

When you are choosing a dating partner, two very powerful laws are working for and against you at the same time. The law of "opposites attract" inclines you toward a balanced life—to an extent. It is important, as you move forward in life, to surround yourself with people who bring new perspectives and keep you sharp. If, however, you are attempting to partner with a person who has an *extreme* difference in his or her background, values, beliefs, and interests from you, you are treading on dangerous ground. These relationships rarely work in the end.

The law of "likes attract" (or birds of a feather flock together) also works in your life and can have a positive or negative impact. It is good to connect with people who have similar values, backgrounds, beliefs, and interests as you, since this helps to keep you on your journey rather than pull you off course.

A problem occurs when you connect with people with whom you share common hurts and pains. You get stuck in your hurting histories, which serves to keep both of you down rather than lifted up.

Optimally, you will choose dating partners who bring commonality and diversity, utilizing both the laws of "likes attract" and "opposites attract."

Remember this important factor: you have the power to choose and choose wisely. But no amount of strategies, guidelines, or list making will help you find the man or woman of your dreams unless you decide you deserve it. You *will* attract exactly what you *believe* you want, need, or desire. Nothing will change until you search deep inside, and possibly get some help from an established counselor, to determine why you draw the wrong people into your life.

GETTING HELP

There is help out there for combating the false assumptions we make. For some reason, many of us think we can figure out relationship issues ourselves and we fail to take advantage of the tools available to help us make healthy relationship choices. True, we have the ability to reason, but if we'll just access resources such as relationship and marriage books, classes, seminars, and professionals, we'll find help for areas where we may be lacking expertise.

The person with whom you decide to spend your life hugely impacts your level of happiness, contentment, and success. It's almost impossible to truly be happy if you are unhappy in your marriage. How many married people have learned to put on smiling faces and act happy, but when the outer layers are peeled away, they are filled with loneliness and resentment?

Getting help with relationships offers many rewards and payoffs. Unhappily married and single people on the average suffer more physical ailments, more frequent periods of loneliness, and lower self-esteem, which leads to higher incidents of depression, anxiety, insomnia, suicide, and drug addiction. These people also tend to harbor more anger and resentment. Happily married people report more satisfaction in life. Overall they experience better physical health and on average outlive those who are not happily married.

A December 15, 2004 WebMD Medical News article cited a news release by the Centers for Disease Control and Prevention (1999-2002). The CDC examined over 127,000 adults between 1999 and 2000. The study indicated married people are healthier than those who are divorced, widowed, never-married, or living with a partner. Here are some of the findings:

- Across the board, married persons were healthier for nearly every measure of health. That was true for all ages, ethnicities, and levels of income and education.

- The connection between marriage and health was strongest in the youngest group, ages 18-44.
- Married people were less likely to suffer from health conditions like back pain, headaches, and serious psychological distress.
- Married people were also less likely to smoke, drink heavily, and be physically inactive. For instance, married men and women under age 44 were about half as likely to be current smokers.

Living with someone did not confer the same benefits as being married. People with live-in partners didn't match the health of married adults. Instead, they were more like divorced or separated people in terms of health.

Reality Check

What healthy decisions have you made in relationships, and how have they positively affected your life?

What unhealthy decisions have you made in relationships, and how have they negatively affected your life?

Write It Down

Make your wish list of *every* positive quality you *want* in a mate, including physical, emotional, behavioral, cultural/geographical, financial, occupational, educational, familial, recreational, age, and previous-relationship status (married, kids, and so forth).

Make your list of *every* negative quality you have experienced (or hope not to experience) in a relationship, including physical, emotional, behavioral, cultural/geographical, financial, occupational, educational, familial, recreational, age, and previous-relationship status (married, kids, and so forth).

Where do you picture your life in the following areas in five, ten, twenty years?

• Family Married, with 2-4 children or at least on the way, nice house in nice neighborhood.

• Work Graduated FWBBC with a great teaching job.

• Leisure having a boat would be nice. :(

What is your definition of love?
Someone you feel a deep connection with that you can share life goals & dreams, you feel can complement you in every way.

Do your goals as a couple match or at least complement each other's? How do you intend to reach those goals?
Yes they do. Reach them by helping each other.

If your goals are different, how can you support each other's goals without compromising a future marital relationship?

(2)

It Takes Three Loves

Singles say…

>…they don't want to meet someone in a bar.

>…they flatter a potential partner to gain interest.

>…they use the sense of touch to engage a potential dating partner.

>…they meet more quality dates when their friends set them up.

As a teenager, Jack spent summers working on his dad's farm. When Jack's dad sent him to find a tool, he would sometimes have no clue what he was looking for. Rather than asking his dad to describe the tool, he would mill around the shop trying to figure it out himself. When Jack didn't return for a while, his dad would usually arrive and walk straight to the tool in question. Jack's dad ultimately fired him. Looking back, Jack says, "It was absurd that I spent time looking through toolboxes when I didn't even know what I was looking for. How would I have even known if I found it?"

Amazingly, millions of people look for their mates in the same haphazard way Jack searched for tools in his dad's shop. They don't even know what type of person they are looking for, but somehow they believe they will positively know it when they find the right one. "I'll feel it," they say.

"Feel what?" you might ask.

"Love!" everyone answers.

The next question ought to be, "Do you really know what love is?"

WHAT IS LOVE?

Foreigner, a popular '80s rock band, recorded a number-one hit called "I Want to Know What Love Is." The first line of the chorus goes, "I want to know what love is; I want you to show me." You might guess the lead singer was not making that statement to a counselor.

Love is the foundation of the relationship with your life mate, but what does that really look like? The word *love* is used so loosely in the English language, it can mean many different things: You can love your dog, but that's different from the way you love your mother (at least let's hope so). You can love a song, a child, and spring days, and you can even score love in

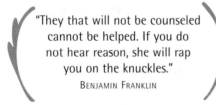

"They that will not be counseled cannot be helped. If you do not hear reason, she will rap you on the knuckles."
BENJAMIN FRANKLIN

tennis. You can love a friend, a job, fried chicken, and God. You can also love the person you're dating.

The word *love* can represent very different emotions. So what sets apart the emotion we have toward a future husband or wife from warm feelings we have for friends and family members? After all, romantic love is supposed to be a unique type of love, isn't it? Learning more about how feelings work will help you understand how relationships begin and eventually progress to the point where both people desire a lifetime commitment.

Let's pause to consider Jay's story—an example of what can go wrong when life-altering decisions are made based on an incomplete understanding of real love.

Jay and three of his buddies celebrated the completion of their first year of medical school with a Caribbean cruise. Four guys left from the airport to board the ship in Florida. A week later only three returned. Jay was missing. (No, he didn't fall overboard.) Jay met Tina, from New York City, who had accompanied her cousin on the same cruise in celebration of the cousin's recent divorce. (Perhaps that should have raised a red flag for Jay.) After the second night of the cruise Jay and Tina were inseparable. He changed his return flight in order to go to New York with her. Several days later the new couple returned to Jay's place in her car, with the trunk and backseat loaded with clothes. She was moving in.

Jay said he knew from the first night he met Tina that she was the person he was supposed to marry. "You don't understand how I feel around her. It is a love like I have never known!"

Jay's warm and fuzzy feeling was likely caused by a testosterone surge due to physical attraction combined with a six-hour "deep" conversation he had with her in the moonlight. Everything "just clicked," he said. In reality, he didn't really know Tina yet. She might well have been the one, but he took no time to find out more about her.

His friends pleaded with him not to make a spur-of-the-moment marriage decision, but Jay didn't take their advice and instead walked the aisle after knowing Tina barely more than a month.

Life sailed smoothly over the summer for the new couple, but when medical school resumed in August, the warm fuzzy feeling started fading. Tina couldn't stand being alone during the day while Jay attended classes and studied. She also resented living on a shoestring budget, which is obligatory for most medical students. Tina supposedly spent her days looking for a job at nearby malls and clothing stores, and though she never found a job, she did manage to max out Jay's credit cards.

She also befriended another young lady, and the two began frequenting the city's bar and nightclub scene. Rumors about their adventures began to filter through the medical school. One afternoon Jay came home to their apartment and all of her belongings were gone—with a note from Tina explaining how life with him was not for her anymore. She and her new friend were headed somewhere more exciting to live. Suddenly, Jay's warm fuzzy feeling was gone, and so was his student loan money after Tina emptied his bank account. Tina was nice enough to give back the wedding ring. Jay wanted to pawn it, but his friends told him to keep it as a reminder of his foolishness.

Jay had thought he was in love—and he was. What he felt is one form of love, but it was a love based on physical and/or emotional feeling. Feelings are fickle. They change like the wind. They're hard to control. People who base major life decisions on feelings usually are making unstable decisions.

In order to fully understand what love is, it's important to recognize that there are several types of love. The ancient Greeks identified at least three types: eros, philos, and agape. Each type of love has its own distinctive depth and meaning. *Philos* and *agape* are words frequently mentioned in the Bible, but the word *eros* is only encountered in secular literature of the period. Modern-day counselors, whether of the Christian faith or not, often use these terms in their practices to distinguish exactly "what love is" for clients. Let's explore each term in detail.

Eros Love

The word *erotic* has its root in the Greek word *eros*. Eros identifies passionate love combined with sensual desire. Physical attraction and sexual attraction drive erotic love, which can develop quickly and feel overwhelmingly strong. Numerous teenagers who are "in love" are experiencing this form. Some people describe eros as "chemistry" or "fate" or even "love at first sight."

Many of the physical sensations accompanying eros are derived from a small part of the brain called the hypothalamus, the section that controls hormone levels. New couples in love experience eros as a hormone surge every time they see each other. This phase may last up to 18 months. Eros can also turn on and off and be activated or deactivated. For instance, physical illness, anger, stress, or even bad breath can deactivate eros. Romantic evenings, vacations, and togetherness spark it again. For the most part, however, this type of love eventually gives way under the everydayness of life.

Do not think that physical attraction *always* means "sex." What is meant in terms of eros is that those initial feelings of attraction—*whatever* they may be—are ruling you. You may not be attracted by looks but instead by intelligence or power or even scent. Whatever triggers that eros response in you needs to be kept in check, so try to stay on top of controlling this phenomenon by understanding its effect on you.

"You must look into people, as well as at them."
LORD CHESTERFIELD

What factors trigger eros? Largely our five senses: sight, sound, smell, touch, and taste. Much of this happens subconsciously, which means you're not even aware that it's occurring.

Sight: Sight has a powerful influence on a male. Simply seeing the body of a female can turn on a guy. Women, on the other hand, do not get many thrills from viewing the average male body. (This helps explain why pornography, a multi-billion-dollar industry, is driven principally by males.) Colors also evoke pleasurable feelings and often mirror moods of the people wearing them.

Sound: Sounds can be soothing, like waterfalls, or frightening, like the howl of a wolf. Just as the sounds of nature bring about certain emotions, many clients report that the sounds of some people bring them pleasure—or discomfort. The pitch of a person's voice, accent, or speed at which he or she speaks all prompt feelings. Thankfully, there are different strokes for different folks. A voice that sounds gruff to you may be sweet music to another's ear.

Smell: Smell exerts an extremely powerful effect on our emotions. It is the only one of our five senses processed directly by the hypothalamus, the region of the brain that regulates sexual libido. This explains why perfume manufacturing is a multi-billion-dollar worldwide industry. Why will a woman spend a hundred dollars for a small bottle of perfume? She recognizes—at some level—the power of smell.

Why do men buy roses for their sweethearts? Because the smell entices her. Why does every gas station sell breath mints? Because halitosis is a powerful repulsing agent. Smells are also strongly linked to emotions and memories. Have you ever walked into a house that smells like your grandmother's?

> "The trouble with most of us is that we would rather be ruined by praise than saved by criticism."
> NORMAN VINCENT PEALE

What emotions were uncovered? Have you visited a high-school cafeteria? Did it remind you of your past? Have you ever eaten so much pizza you became nauseated? Even though you love pizza, what happened the next time you smelled it?

Touch: Soft skin, silky hair, toned muscles, warm hands—all these evoke pleasurable feelings. Holding hands, hugging, and kissing are all forms of touching. Touching activates eros, but it can also quell it. Pushing, hitting, or any form of physical abuse can destroy eros. So can the lack of touch. Some people are more touchy-feely than others. Much has to do with the sort of family in which you were raised. Someone too touchy can turn some people off, while someone too standoffish can leave others wanting.

Taste: Taste is closely tied to our sense of smell. It, too, plays a role in emotions and feelings toward others. Teenage girls love to maximize the effect of taste by wearing strawberry and bubble-gum lip gloss (and boys love to sample the taste on their lips!). Eating ice cream or chocolate with your loved one can also be a strong eros activator, whereas a big bowl of sauerkraut is probably not.

Eros love is important to share with your life mate, but you certainly shouldn't make your marriage decision based on something so transitory. That would be like shopping for a house, finding a newly painted one with a fragrant flower garden, and deciding to buy it without ever looking inside. The house might not have running water, or it might be infested with rats. It will likely fail to meet your expectations. The wise person says, "This house has my attention, so I'll stop and examine it further." Then he or she begins the process of ensuring the internal structure and beauty match the original perception based on outside appearances.

Eros is only a starting point in a romantic relationship. The good news about eros is that it spurs people to pursue a relationship further. The bad news is that it might lead a couple into deep trouble—the kind that happened to Jay when he acted on impulse, got married in a hurry, and soon regretted it.

Philos Love

Philos is a Greek word that has been translated "brotherly love" and is found throughout the Bible. Here are just a few examples:

- If one falls down, his friend can help him up. But pity the man who falls and has no one to help him up! (Ecclesiastes 4:10)

- And when she finds it, she calls her friends and neighbors together and says, "Rejoice with me; I have found my lost coin." (Luke 15:9)
- Greater love has no one than this, that he lay down his life for his friends. (John 15:13)

Philos is the type of love you share with a close friend, and it develops after spending substantial time with someone whose company you enjoy. It's less feeling-based and more stable than eros. Philos love is extremely important in finding your life mate, but it is not the key factor. You can "philos love" your teammates, coworkers, your next-door neighbor, and even your golfing buddy, but you don't necessarily have a desire to marry any of them.

"There are two primary choices in life: to accept conditions as they exist, or accept the responsibility for changing them."
Dr. Denis Waitley

What factors lead to philos love? Rather than responding to the physical senses, it develops as each person's character traits and interests become known to the other; if conditions are favorable, this can lead to long-term compatibility and might contribute to lasting love.

Philos is discovered as a couple spends time together—going out to eat, watching movies, hanging out with friends. What characteristics do they see in each other that draw them together? Is it looks, charm, wit, knowledge, empathy, or sympathy, or something more sinister like wallet size? Although these attributes may prompt their initial interest in each other, it's something more subconscious that keeps them interested.

We grow to philos love someone because we like ourselves when we are around that person. We long for the company of people who make us feel good about ourselves.

You may go out with a handsome man and find your eros turned on by him, but he may be arrogant, and that dries up your desire to be in his company. When philos love fails to develop, the relationship usually crumbles. Negative, overly critical, and pessimistic people are harder to philos love. Why? Because few of us feel better about ourselves after spending a few hours with a constant complainer. It's easy to become more negative and critical yourself when hanging around someone else who is. This often happens subconsciously, leaving others to point out our behavior to us.

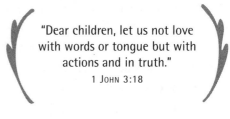

"Dear children, let us not love with words or tongue but with actions and in truth."
1 JOHN 3:18

In counseling practices, we generally see philos developing after eros in males. Conversely, females will sometimes make statements such as, "He grew on me." They're describing how romantic feeling, eros, surfaced after a period of friendship, philos.

Philos is what creates day-to-day enjoyment in a marriage. A marriage missing philos is usually a cold marriage. It may look normal in public, but at home the partners treat each other like detached roommates. What turns off philos? Anger, resentment, distrust, selfishness, arrogance, and even self-pity.

Agape Love

Agape love is the most difficult type of love to describe. In the Christian interpretation, it means Christlike love. The Bible explains that husbands are to love their wives as Christ loves His church. Jesus loves His church so much that He sacrificed His own life for it. Jesus' relationship with the church is compared to a marriage, with Jesus as the bridegroom and His believers as the bride. Whether or not a person ascribes to the Christian faith is irrelevant for understanding this concept. Total sacrifice—other-love over self-love—is the key.

Agape love is the deepest form of love a person can have for another, and it takes the longest to develop. However, once turned on, true agape love never turns off. Agape love is the concrete in the foundation of a relationship that lasts for life.

When you agape love someone, you put his or her needs before yours. An example of agape love is that of two people going down in an airplane with one parachute between them, and each saying to the other, "You take the parachute." It is commitment to the point of laying down your life for the other, if necessary.

But wait a minute. You can also have agape love for people you would never intend to marry. Most parents have agape love for their children (except perhaps during the kids' teenage years). You can even develop agape love for a dear friend.

THREE LOVES

So how do these three descriptions of love help you determine which person you should marry? How does love for that special person differ from the way we love others?

The one you marry should be that one person with whom you experience all three types of love. Families can have philos and agape love, but not eros. A serious early-stage dating relationship can have both eros and philos, but not agape. There are numerous two-way combinations of love for another person, but the three-way combination should be reserved for the person you marry. Does this mean you love that person more than God or your parents? No, it means you love that person differently.

But love is love, right? That's like saying food is food. Filet mignon is certainly different from a baloney sandwich. Sadly the English language has one word for love. We attempt to describe love by including adjectives, ending up with "puppy love," "true love," "burning love," or even "madly in love," but these still don't do justice in defining such an encompassing term. Love is a noun, a verb, and an adjective. Is love a feeling or a fact? Is it a privilege or a duty? It is all of these, and more. Love decides what kind of life you will live and what kind of difference you will make in the lives of others. Love is the only thing you can give away and never run out of.

> "People are very open-minded about new things—as long as they're exactly like the old ones."
> CHARLES KETTERING

A happy marriage should comprise a man and woman who are sexually attracted to each other. These two should also be trusted friends—each other's closest friend of the opposite sex. Both should also be committed to the point of sacrificing their lives for each other if ever necessary. Before you consider marrying someone, a good question to ask is, "Would I be willing to give my life for this person?" If the answer is no, it does not necessarily mean this person is not a person you should marry, but rather this is not a person you should marry *now*. If your answer is yes, does your partner feel the same about you? If not, then again consider that this is not the time to marry.

Realize also that sexual attraction can come and go. In some cases it dries up completely. Two married people won't be friends all the time either. But the commitment of sacrifice should be there whether you've been married two weeks or twenty years.

So if you've found the person who fits all these criteria, then it's time to go reserve the church or schedule that talk with her father, right? Hold on! We're just getting started. Love is the most important aspect and base of any successful marriage, but it is not the only factor. Read on.

Reality Check

What triggers an eros response in you?

His touch, the way he smells, the way he kisses me ☺

In your past relationships, which of these triggers have blinded you to possible obstacles in other areas?

The kiss, because other than that there wasn't anything to our relationship.

How would you define the "perfect friend"? Who is a same-gender friend who meets your definition? Someone I can always confide in, have fun & do crazy things with, listens to me, holds me accountable. Rikki & Stephanie Whitt.

Which of your dating partners fit all of your "eros criteria," as well as your "perfect-friend criteria"? Compare your dating partners to your same-gender perfect friend. Do they match fairly closely the perfect-friend definition? Brandon. Yes in both ways.

If any of your dating partners did not fit all your perfect-friend criteria, what caused you to continue the relationship?

I think just not wanting to be alone, having that person around made me feel better.

Write It Down

What are your "must have" eros factors in a mate?

Great personality, smells & looks nice, clean cut, good kisser.

What are your "must have" philos factors in a mate?

Well great personality, good Godly character well behaved, accountablity partner.

What behaviors turn off your eros response?

Burping, Bad breath, acting stupid, gum smacking, smacking while eating.

What behaviors turn off your philos response?

Gossip, being too critical, ignorance.

(3)

Know Yourself

Singles say…

> …they would be willing to take a few weeks to work on themselves
> for the sake of a healthier relationship.
>
> …they believe their poor choices come from lack of self-esteem.
>
> …they can track bad relationships back to faulty perceptions of the
> person or situations.

By now you've probably begun to see patterns in your past relationships that have or have not produced your desired results. You might be wondering about how to use this information to get the healthy, happy relationship you desire. This is where you begin—by looking at yourself first.

You have to work on your own shortcomings before you can deal with someone else's. You must know both your strengths and weaknesses. The person who only knows his own strengths is proud and arrogant. The person who only knows his own weaknesses is the perpetual helpless victim. The person who only knows the weaknesses of others, or plays on the flaws of others to meet his or her own needs, is someone you want to steer clear of. Your goal is to become as healthy as possible before you select a mate so you can see more clearly and make healthy decisions for your future.

Let's start by taking a look at how your actions are connected to your innermost thoughts and emotions. After all, it is our *actions* that may threaten to destroy our dreams, our relationships, and sometimes our very futures. What determines the actions we take in life? Our actions are determined by a combination of our thoughts and emotions. If you're at an ocean beach, for instance, you might consider going in the water, but your thoughts and emotions will determine whether or not you will actually do it. If seeing the ocean evokes the emotion of fear, then you will probably not get wet. If the ocean brings up pleasurable memories and expectations of cool water, then you will likely jump in.

> "He who knows others is learned; he who knows himself is wise."
> LAO-TZE

You can see how two vastly different reactions to the ocean could be based on experiences, memories, and feelings. Many thoughts and emotions are based on life experiences. A memory is actually both a thought and an emotion. We think of something that has happened to us, and that memory is given an emotional tag— pleasurable, fearful, exciting, and so on.

Emotions are actually produced in the brain, even though the heart has been treated as the seat of emotions by poets and lovers. Emotions also mature as we age. Young children generally have a limited number of emotions, and they have a limited ability to know when it is and is not proper to display those emotions. Adults not only have more complex emotions, but they ought to have better control over these emotions and better insight into their emotions.

Emotions can be misguided, and they can be based on faulty or wrong thinking. For example, people with paranoia believe irrationally that others are out to harm them. So, in turn, fearful emotions produced from these thoughts can lead to bizarre behaviors. Emotions can be immature as well. Immature emotions lead to inconsistent and unpredictable behavior.

EMOTIONAL MATURITY

Benjamin Franklin said, "There are only two things in life you can be sure of—death and taxes." Actually there is a third thing, which is that emotionally unhealthy people are magnets for other emotionally unhealthy people. Once you're in a destructive relationship, it takes an enormous amount of time and effort to correct the trouble.

Before trying to discern if others are emotionally mature, you must make sure your own emotions are mature enough to handle a long-term relationship. Most people rely on feedback from their family members and friends to help pinpoint their own maturity, but the opinions of close friends and relatives could be biased. People sometimes erroneously equate being levelheaded or having intelligence with emotional maturity. But think about it—many serial killers have been both levelheaded and intelligent, but they are certainly emotionally stunted.

Remember that emotional health encompasses not only your own state of mind, but also your ability to spot the healthy or dysfunctional emotional status of others. You may be personally capable of maintaining healthy relationships but still be unable to recognize dysfunction in others. We usually call this naïveté. If you struggle with identifying unhealthy people, your struggle could stem from the belief that everyone has the same mind-set as you. That's usually not the case, however. Remember, if you recognize you're with a dysfunctional person and stick with him or her anyway, you might be in for years of chaos, conflict, and heartache.

Emotional maturity is an important element because if you are emotionally immature, you will not be able to spot the person who would be best for you to date and potentially marry. The story of Cricket and Jake shows the upside of what can happen when emotional-health issues are recognized and dealt with aggressively.

Cricket and Jake came from vastly different family backgrounds. Jake's was a conservative, close-knit, fairly functional family. Cricket's parents had several divorces between them as well as a variety of ongoing dysfunctional behaviors. Cricket decided long ago to overcome her family's dysfunction and pursue the life she wished she'd had growing up. Cricket did not just talk, but she worked hard to use her past to shape a different future for herself. When she had done as much work as she could to change her life and herself for the better—including undergoing years of counseling—she met her Prince Charming—Jake.

Everything Jake was personally as well as his family of origin met the standards she set for herself in creating a new and different family life. She was honest with Jake about her background, and he respected her for the goals she had set for herself. Though Jake felt he had everything together, he took Cricket's lead and went to counseling. Jake learned that in order to have a relationship with a woman who came from a totally different background from his, he would have to constantly use healthy communication skills. While many couples get lazy in this area, Jake's agreement to stay on top of issues, including weekly couple meetings, actually enhanced his life in a way he never anticipated. In spite of his near-perfect family background, he learned that even near-perfection can be improved upon.

The couple married and continued working on these issues, becoming healthy and happy within their marriage and family. They have moved forward with their individual purposes and complement each other well as an active married couple.

Here are some questions to help you determine your own level of emotional maturity. Answering honestly will also help you in your pursuit of excellent dating partners.

Do you have healthy, productive relationships? How long does your average dating relationship last? Which party usually ends the relationship? Do you change friends a lot or keep the same ones for years? Do you get your feelings hurt easily? When a friend or date hurts you, do you often try to even the score? Do people seem comfortable around you, or is it more like they're "walking on eggshells"?

Do you have two-way, open communication in your relationships? Are disagreements and/or arguments rare or commonplace in your close relationships? When you do have an argument, do you stay mad for several days or get over it quickly? Is there a lot of unfair fighting such as yelling, name-calling, false accusations, and so on? Are you able to resolve most of your disagreements quickly? Are you able to compromise? Are the types of people you date able to compromise? Do you feel free to state your opinion even if it differs from the opinions of others?

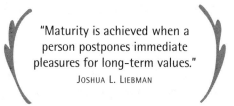

"Maturity is achieved when a person postpones immediate pleasures for long-term values."
JOSHUA L. LIEBMAN

Can you spot a bad relationship before it gets too deep? Have past relationships ended in a friendly way or on bitter terms? Can you accurately look at flaws in someone and determine if they are minor (an irritating habit) or deal-breakers (e.g., you are always to blame for everything)?

PERSONALITY TRAITS

To help you develop a deeper understanding of yourself, let's examine a few personality traits that can enhance or damage a long-term relationship.

Assertiveness vs. Aggressiveness

Are you assertive or aggressive? Assertiveness is good. It allows a person to take a stand on personal convictions while continuing to consider the needs of others. It indicates the courage to be honest and open about what you need, want, and desire from the other person. Assertive people also strive to meet the needs, wants, and desires of their partners.

Aggressiveness, in contrast, is damaging. Aggressive people often demand that their needs, wants, and desires be fulfilled first with little concern for their partners. They use different means to do this, ranging from subtle manipulation to violent force. Aggressive people are insecure deep down, though they may come across on the surface as having it all together. Usually the more insecure they grow, the more jealous, demanding, and dominating they become. You may be thinking, *Who in the world would stay in a relationship with someone like that?* Another insecure person. That's why self-esteem is so important, as you'll see a bit later in this chapter.

> "Before you begin climbing that ladder of success, make sure it's leaning toward the window of opportunity you desire."
> TRACY BRINKMANN

How do you become more assertive?

Say no when necessary. This may take some practice, but do it. People who say yes to too many requests can become worn out and start resenting the people they intended to help. Additionally, if they are spread too thin, their help will not live up to the recipients' expectations.

Set firm boundaries. We all have limitations, so why not let them be known? Relationships bloom when both partners can freely express their own boundaries while respecting the other's boundaries. You might want to read the book *Boundaries* by Drs. John Townsend and Henry Cloud; it's one of the classic books of our time about relationships and a must read for anyone considering marriage.

Openly seek to clarify issues. How many needless conflicts arise from simply misunderstanding each other? Even though you may laugh about the misunderstanding later, the anger it causes at the time can damage the relationship. Handling issues assertively rather than aggressively will strengthen not only intimate relationships, but *all* your relationships. Your life will change when you realize how much positive influence you can have in relationships by knowing how to better handle the issues that arise.

No two people think or act exactly the same; therefore, every relationship will produce friction. We drive our cars daily and rarely think about the engine until it is time to change the oil every three or four thousand miles. Without the motor oil present to reduce friction in the engine, our cars would overheat and blow up. Many motor oils today make your engine more efficient while preserving its life. Think of your efforts to handle issues effectively—through assertiveness—as high-quality oil.

Failing to act assertively when problems arise increases the likelihood of fomenting aggressiveness. Aggressiveness may not kill a relationship instantly, but it's just a matter of time before the affected relationship explodes. Assertive action, on the other hand, controls a situation before it gets out of hand, much like a small campfire can be easily extinguished so it doesn't become a forest fire that destroys everything in its path.

High Self-esteem vs. Low Self-esteem

How would you rate your self-esteem: low, average, high, or extremely high? What level of self-esteem should your partner have? How will your and your partner's self-esteem impact your relationship?

Self-esteem can have an enormous impact on a marriage relationship. Mismatched self-esteem between partners will generally erode the relationship. People with low self-esteem suffer more sadness and depression, tend to be needier, and experience more jealousy and possessiveness in relationships. They also report less satisfaction overall in their dating and marriage relationships.

People with low self-esteem usually experience a higher rate of failed relationships. Sometimes the behavior stemming from their own insecurities (about losing the relationship) is what dooms the relationship. People who don't feel good about themselves can often misread the intentions and actions

> "That's the risk you take if you change, that people you've been involved with won't like the new you. But other people who do will come along."
> LISA ALTHER

of others. People with poor self-worth also are less able to assertively express their needs, wants, and desires in a relationship. Why? Because deep down they feel that they don't deserve to have them met. When this happens, they often assume a passive role in the relationship, then feel like victims when things don't go their way. This type of person frequently makes false accusations about a partner, making the partner the perpetual bad guy.

Self-esteem is largely determined during childhood and adolescence. When children are continually put down, not allowed to express their feelings, or simply ignored, they develop a deeply ingrained sense of inferiority. Adolescents' experiences in school also play a large role in the development of their self-esteem.

The good news about self-esteem is that it can be changed for the better. Does having a steady boyfriend or girlfriend improve self-esteem? Never. Expecting a boyfriend or girlfriend to do this for you is dangerous. Improving your self-esteem starts with *you*. Your self-worth is your responsibility. Even though you may not be the sole cause of its being where it is today, you are the one responsible to change it. A good first step is to find a qualified counselor who can help shed light on how your life events have shaped your self-image. At first you may have no idea how your self-image developed, but an astute counselor can soon uncover vital clues to your personality.

Further good news is that you're not responsible for anyone else's level of self-worth. Thinking that it's your responsibility to change someone else's self-esteem can be a setup for failure. Some insecure people may try to make you feel responsible for their happiness or misery. These types of relationships are often frustrating for both partners.

What about the opposite? What is it like to date someone with an extremely high self-esteem? High self-esteem is not generally a problem. But don't confuse high self-esteem with an unhealthy, overactive ego.

Ego-driven people often look for dating partners with poor self-worth, because they usually can't sustain a relationship with those as ego driven as they are. Why? Because it begins to expose the truth that they really feel inferior. They need to feel in control at all times. If you choose someone like this, you will be expected to accept the role of being in the "one down" position. Also don't be surprised if friends and family don't care to hang out with you as a couple or extend you invitations.

The best combination is two people with healthy high self-esteem. Both are confident enough to stand alone, without dependence on each other, but each is humble enough to admit wrongs and work on areas of weakness. If you have poor self-esteem, don't just endure it. Change it. It will make all the difference in your life and the life of the person you choose to marry.

Externalizes vs. Internalizes

Are you an externalizer or an internalizer? Externalizers look outside themselves for contentment and purpose. Other people and circumstances control their well-being. An unhappy externalizer starts looking for someone to blame and invariably points the finger at those closest to him or her. Externalizers say things like, "My life is unhappy because you talk to other men," or, "If you'd only treat me with more respect, we could have a good relationship." When an externalizer experiences failure, it is never his or her own fault, but rather the fault of others.

Internalizers take responsibility for their own lives. When an internalizer feels down, rather than placing blame, he or she will focus on doing something to facilitate feeling better. An externalizer who gains a hundred pounds eating fast food every day blames the fast-food restaurant for his predicament. He may even sue. An internalizer who gains a hundred pounds from frequent fast-food feasts realizes the food was not healthy, but acknowledges he chose to consume it. Reasoning that suing McDonald's won't help his weight predicament, he takes responsibility for finding appropriate avenues such as exercising and improving his diet to shed weight.

Externalizers tend to be depressed and have a great deal of dissatisfaction with life. They also have little joy within their partner relationships—or any relationship for that matter.

The majority of internalizers have much more happiness in life as well as overall relationship satisfaction. The small number of internalizers who do report depression and relationship difficulty are the ones who take it too far, meaning they take responsibility for problems they did not cause. While generally internalizers have a healthier perspective on their problems and work to solve them, in the extreme they can suffer guilt and condemnation for problems as vast as world hunger.

LOOKING BACK: HOW DID YOU GET WHERE YOU ARE?

Why is the past important? While dwelling too much on history may keep you rooted in past hurts or happiness or prohibit you from creating a positive future, you should study your history so you might understand how you got to where you are, avoid making the same mistakes, and continue doing things that work for you. As Dr. Phil says: "How's that working for you?" Use this oft-quoted question as you consider your own history.

While the person you marry wields a powerful effect on your life (more than any other human), you should take responsibility for fulfilling your own purpose and finding happiness in life. If you leave that responsibility to someone else, you are "overexpecting." Overexpecting will leave you chronically disappointed. If you blame another for your disappointment, the relationship will soon be brimming with resentment. Examine your life, and attempt to analyze if you are truly fulfilling your purpose. If you are, you are probably fairly content. If you are waiting on someone else to make your life meaningful and happy, you will almost certainly be gravely disappointed.

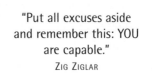

"Put all excuses aside and remember this: YOU are capable."
ZIG ZIGLAR

Tara's story provides a good example of a young woman who didn't know herself well enough when she starting dating. Her lack of insight led her into a situation of overexpectation that was difficult to escape.

Tara and Guy were lifelong friends and high-school sweethearts. They became engaged and set a wedding date but decided not to marry until they had graduated from college, bought a house, and landed solid jobs. Both came from successful but somewhat dysfunctional families, in that they never let relationships get in the way of what they needed to do. Although somewhat unhealthy, the family relationships were steady for most of their lives.

During college and after graduation, Tara's friends began to notice she was becoming demanding and self-centered. She was also growing more and more emotional, draining everyone's energy. Daily, Tara made multiple calls to her friends, asking them to help rescue her from the turmoil of her relationship with Guy. Individually, her friends began to realize that for three years their old friend Tara had shown no interest in their lives and had given no support to them in times of trouble.

Quite understandably, Tara's friends began to drop out of her life. Tara was so self-absorbed, she did not see this coming or even notice it—even when she only had one real friend left.

During these years, Guy frequently contacted Tara's friends and relatives to convince them that Tara was "out of control." Of course, the behaviors Guy described matched their own observations. Just before Tara's last friend was hours away from jumping ship, Tara called with the news that for the last time, she had allowed Guy to threaten a breakup. It was the last time because Tara called him on it and gave back the ring.

To everyone's surprise, Tara returned to the person she once was. Almost immediately her friends and family began to realize that rather than complementing Tara, Guy was merely using her to work out his sick control games. His manipulating and controlling behavior was actually enhancing the worst qualities in Tara, and that served his purpose in always having chaos in his life, which mirrored his own family life during his childhood. Tara went through counseling for over a year and worked through the relationship and personal issues that had contributed to her dysfunctional relationship with Guy.

Guy had thought he had control over Tara and that she would never call his bluff. When she did, it was a wake-up call to him. Though Guy and Tara had no contact for over a year, Tara did finally take a phone call from him. He admitted everything he had done and stated, "I turned into my father." He begged to make things work and promised to go to counseling as well. The two of them went to counseling, but Tara finally made the decision not to return to a relationship with Guy. He changed in every positive way, but Tara knew that because she had set up a relationship where she had allowed him to emotionally abuse her for years, the potential existed for both of them to fall back into that old trap. They parted ways amicably, and Tara counted it as a hard but worthwhile lesson. Guy, on the other hand, counted it as a loss he never expected to suffer.

RESTARTING IN THE MIDDLE

Tara eventually recovered her identity after attempting to change her relationship with Guy midstream. What she failed to do at first was establish healthy boundaries—those internal lines that clearly separate one's self, feelings, decisions, needs, and so forth from those of another person. As Tara eventually learned, the best way to launch a healthy relationship is to start with healthy boundaries. But what about existing relationships like that of Tara and Guy, which started off with poor or marginal boundaries? Can you actually go back and restart a relationship already in progress?

You can't make another person change, but you can change yourself. That will change the dynamics of the relationship—by improving it or possibly ending it. The relationship may actually get worse before it gets better, because when you start setting healthy boundaries, those who know you best are going to be thrown for a loop and may even feel threatened. Your significant other could respond positively right off the bat when you set boundaries, but be aware he or she might instead resist the new healthy you. This could happen the first day of your changed behavior or after three weeks, when you think all is well. Clinicians know to warn clients that the relationship could get worse before it gets better. How do you handle this? By continuing to keep on doing what you are doing. Consistency is the key to success with behavior changes, especially in relationships. Your relationship should be able to withstand positive changes. If it doesn't, that is a sure sign you may need to rethink your partner as a potential life mate.

KEEP YOUR BALANCE

As you discover, rediscover, or work to change yourself, you'll hopefully be less likely to become involved in an unhealthy relationship, because you'll see that it's not fitting into your new view of life. No more impulsive jumping into a relationship and allowing it to consume you. When you maintain your new sense of balance, any relational debris will come flying out fast.

If you've been a people person who gets easily sucked into unhealthy dependent relationships, do your charity work with people you're not in relationship with in order to get your "fix" of helping others. Do not allow a dependent or needy person into your personal life. Do not marry one or make one your best friend. Ministering to someone is healthy, but doing so while married to or in deep friendship with him or her is unhealthy for both of you. You may not want to hurt someone's feelings by "rejecting" such a relationship, but by allowing a person to suck the energy and life out of you, you are negatively affecting yourself and the life you want. Be wise with your relationships, and don't get in so deeply in a dependent one that you cannot get out.

> "Brothers, each man, as responsible to God, should remain in the situation God called him to."
> 1 CORINTHIANS 7:24

A horse expert was describing the yoke that a team of horses wears when it pulls a large object. She stated that the purpose of the yoke is to keep the team pulling safely and uniformly. Because of the structure of the yoke, if the weaker horse in the team stumbles, it will always pull down the stronger horse. Relationships respond similarly. Yoke yourself to someone who pulls you down and you will not likely be able to get back up without a lot of pain and damage.

What happens when men and women truly understand themselves before getting involved in a dating relationship? The story of one young couple offers a positive example:

Kelly and Tom were both recovering alcoholics and drug addicts. Though they were fairly young, they had both been through extensive AA meetings and therapy to get to the roots of their own addictions. They had both learned individually about the impact of their dysfunctional families, along with their own personality types, on their addictions. The pair met and felt attracted to each other, but after examining each of their backgrounds, they decided not to pursue a romantic relationship. Wise recovering addicts know it is important not to become involved in relationships that might encourage them to get back into addictive behaviors.

The two could not stop thinking about each other, so they sought counseling before they decided to formally date. Their goal was not to talk themselves into the relationship or fit a square-peg relationship into round-hole lives. They simply felt the relationship might be too good not to at least explore doing it right, and yet they knew it could be destructive for them to connect with each other based on their past histories.

The couple began to explore their past issues in therapy and created a dating plan for their future. They not only followed their plan, but found each other to be a great support for the family issues they both were dealing with. They decided to stay in counseling to keep themselves grounded as a couple and family.

They married, had children, and were actually healthier within their relationship and home life than many couples with more functional backgrounds.

Through assertiveness and healthy boundary setting early on, Kelly and Tom saw the red flags, addressed every one of them head-on, and ended up living happily ever after—past addictions, dysfunctional families, and all. They were able to break many family and personal destructive cycles all because of the healthy way they set up their relationship as a couple.

Reality Check

Do you know your purpose or have a plan for your life? If not, are you at least moving forward?

Can you say no when a person or event threatens to deter you from moving forward in your personal life?

How do you normally respond to those people or events, and what generally happens in the end?

Do you tend to have positive communication with most people?

If not, what will you do in the next three months to work on more positive communication?

Write It Down

Before you proceed in a dating relationship, perform an honest evaluation of yourself by considering the questions that follow.

• Do you consistently blame others for how your life is going?

• Are you blamed or held responsible if your dating partner is not happy?

• Do you have unrealistic expectations in your relationships?

• What about your partner? Do you feel he or she has unrealistic expectations about you?

• Do you feel resentment brewing in your relationship?

If you answered yes to any of these questions, now is the time to address the situation. Some people recognize these types of problems in their relationships before getting married but never deal with them. They believe that ignoring this behavior long enough will somehow make it magically disappear.

Tragically, when ignored, the problems escalate or worsen, and the relationship decays into daily discontentment. The way to deal with them, however, is *outside* the relationship. The problems are based in either you personally, your partner personally, or possibly within the two of you as a couple.

(4)

I'm Still Interested—
Now What?

Singles say…

   …finding common interests with a date increases perceived
      attractiveness.

   …they are open to meeting someone on the Internet.

   …they have been broken up with through the Internet more
      than once.

A great relationship needs more than love; it needs compatibility as well. This is an often-overlooked truth in the "Hollywood version" of finding a mate. Have you ever seen a couple in a soap opera discussing whether or not they were compatible? Perhaps if they did, their TV marriages would fare better. However, what fun would it be to watch a show where people were happy and getting along?

If you think of a relationship as a house, love makes up the foundation, but compatibility forms the walls and roof. Both are extremely important for the house to be complete and stormproof. In colonial times young couples often started off their married life with a two-room house. Usually a second story was built when children arrived, and further additions were made as the family had means. These home additions were built upon the original foundation and walls of the two-room house, so it was extremely important that this foundation be strong enough to withstand the added pressure and weight. It was also vital that the walls of the rooms be compatible.

How can you know if you're compatible with someone? First, you have to know yourself; then you have to know what you're looking for in a person. If you've ever made a big purchase such as a house or a car, you probably understand the importance of knowing what you're looking for. If you contact a Realtor and say you're interested in a house, the Realtor will ask multiple questions to learn specifically what you want. These questions might include price range, location, size, or special amenities desired. Once the Realtor has a clear idea of what you want, the next step is to spend time at a potential house to discover if it is compatible with your needs.

When you find a person in whom you're interested, the next step is spending time with that person to discover if you are compatible. This process is a two-way street—as both people are evaluating their mutual compatibility. You are both addressing the question, "Do we make a good match?"

When it comes to knowing what we're looking for, many of us have compiled our checklists of what we want in a mate. These lists are usually hidden in our heads and contain those traits we desire and also those we reject. In addition, we have a set of questions that we'll ask about the relationship. Let's look at some of these questions.

DO WE HAVE SIMILAR INTERESTS?

A thousand years ago this question was probably of little value in a relationship. Humans spent most of their waking hours working to gather enough food to survive, and most humans rarely traveled more than a few miles from where they were born. My, how times have changed! Today our interests make up a large part of who we are. Some people may have interests similar to yours, but each one of us is different from every other human. Even identical twins have independent interests.

Finding someone with similar interests is a plus in a relationship. People with similar interests often meet in the first place because of those interests. If you enjoy going to weekend horse shows, then you are more likely to meet other people who enjoy horses and these weekend events. Sharing

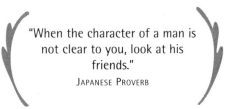

"When the character of a man is not clear to you, look at his friends."
JAPANESE PROVERB

similar interests is convenient at the beginning of a relationship. It provides commonality. You have common subjects to talk about, common activities to participate in, and often a common group of friends.

But what if you start dating someone with different interests from yours? Or you discover that you have some interests that are similar, but many that are different? This is a valid and an important concern. Relationships between two people with different interests can often survive and sometimes even thrive—as long as those differences aren't too extreme. The question people often ask about interests in a relationship is, "How alike are we?" But perhaps the more appropriate question should be, "How different are we?"

Different interests are usually reconcilable. One of you can like action movies while the other one prefers love stories. It's easy to compromise by taking turns choosing movies to watch. Or you might watch a spy thriller with an interwoven love story. New interests can be acquired through this process of compromise as well. You may learn to like new foods, find new hobbies, and even develop new skills that you've never had because someone you're dating introduces you to them. When you think about it, life would be boring if we all shared the exact same interests.

Interests become difficult to reconcile when they're radically different. Tattooing the whole body would be fine with some people but totally unacceptable to others. You might be right at home living in a secluded cabin in the woods with no electricity, but many would consider that to be a radical interest. It's possible to fall in love with a cabin dweller yet find the aspect of establishing a permanent relationship with that person incompatible with your desires.

Interests change during our lives. Sometimes they change directly because of a relationship. You might give up skydiving when you get engaged because you know the dangers frighten your wife-to-be. If you choose to give it up voluntarily, with no pressure from your partner, you will likely be content with your decision. Other interests change because circumstances in your life change. When you're in your fifties, your interests will likely be much different from when you were 20 years old. Your bedtime will likely be earlier, too. Changing interests can work both ways in a relationship— they can bring people closer together or drive them further apart.

Tony started a new job about a year before he and Cleo planned to marry. He had gone on sailing trips with his coworkers a few times and absolutely loved it. These outings also gave Tony a chance to get to know some of his superiors at work and their spouses, opening a chance for him to advance at his current job.

Cleo was desperately afraid of the water. Tony offered to pay for her to take swimming lessons, but she resisted out of fear. Several months later Cleo realized that Tony's interest in sailing was negatively affecting their relationship. She felt lonely and left out whenever he was gone on a sailing trip. Tony always asked Cleo if it was okay with her before he went sailing. Even so, she sensed that when he did stay home, even though they had fun doing other things, he longed to be out on the water.

Cleo considered calling off the wedding because she had serious questions about their compatibility. After talking it over with her sister, she came to terms with the reality that she needed to step up and face her fear of water out of love for Tony. Cleo learned to swim and even enrolled in sailing lessons. She loved her new ability to swim and found sailing a thrill.

Tony was impressed that his fiancée's hard work in learning to swim and sail was a labor of love motivated by wanting to spend more time with him. Now sailing is an interest they enjoy together. It actually strengthened their relationship even more and gave them a whole new group of interesting friends.

HOW WILL WE BALANCE OUR TIME?

Today in a world of communication overload, we can find couples actually spending too much time together, generally to the detriment of each person as well as the long-term couple relationship. Overdependence between couples is rampant today, along with the destruction of healthy boundaries that actually serve to hold a relationship together. Too much time together and commingling common interests to the extreme erodes the boundaries in the areas of work, school, daily responsibilities, and other relationships. Conversely, too little time together leads to shallow relationships and not intimately knowing each other.

The question of how much time is too much or too little with a dating partner is generally asked after this issue has contributed to relationship heartache. Often the problem has less to do with the amount of time spent together, and more to do with a disparity between expectations of time spent together.

Because of the eros factors discussed previously, the temptation is great in the beginning of a relationship to spend every possible moment connecting with your new love, especially when you share common interests. Avoid this temptation at all costs, as it is a setup for relationship problems down the road.

Let's look at how a well-balanced person might allocate his or her weekly time, and then we'll discuss how that can impact your dating relationships.

Hypothetically, allocate the hours in your typical week in the following manner, and for everything listed below, think of not including your dating partner in your schedule. This includes no cell phone calls, text messaging, instant messaging, and so on.

- 56 hours for sleep
- 40 hours for work
- 14 hours for personal business (grocery shopping, paying bills, physician appointments, running errands, pet care, car care, home care, chores, and so on)
- 6 hours visiting or calling family and friends
- 3 hours for exercise
- 3 hours for your hobbies
- 2 hours for religious or charity work

There are 168 hours in each week, and by subtracting the above 124 hours, you are left with 44 hours of free time each week to allocate however you want.

Does that mean you need to be spending 44 hours each week with a potential dating partner? Not necessarily. But first, let's look at what those 124 hypothetical hours *without* your date do for your new relationship as a whole.

Spending 124 hours without your date makes you a more interesting person with lots of conversation topics to cover when you do get together. Additionally, it is unwise to commingle everything in your life with another person. This is called enmeshment, and it is unhealthy. Keeping a separate life gives you constant conversation topics, keeps you strong as an individual, and gives your date lots of things to brag about when telling family and friends about you. Taking care of yourself by setting healthy boundaries and ensuring you stay interesting, balanced, and healthy will actually make your relationship stronger over time. If you have no life, go and get one.

Remember, a relationship is not your destination. It is an enhancement to your life.

A healthy, balanced life of your own will keep you grounded, and you will be able to see red flags as they pop up. Does your dating partner respect your work day, time with friends and family, and separate hobbies? Keeping your own support network and some of your interests separate from this relationship will help you see the person as well as the relationship through clearer eyes.

The other issue here is communication. If you limit your communication and stop texting and messaging constantly, you force the relationship into healthy communication skills from the start. Communication is like many other things—the quality, not the quantity, counts.

Now, let's talk time and interests. Say you met your new dating partner skydiving. This doesn't mean you shouldn't necessarily skydive together; just do it in a balanced way. Keep your old skydiving buddies and continue skydiving with them by yourself. Your boyfriend or girlfriend should do the same. If you

> "If you don't design your own life plan, chances are you'll fall into someone else's plan. And guess what they have planned for you? Not much."
> JIM ROHN

want to go together at times, do it. Just remember, once you start commingling these friends, you begin associating your love of skydiving with your date, and you start making friends who may not remain unbiased if you need a little love advice down the road. Yes, you want to meet each other's friends and family, but keep a healthy handle on the life you had before this person came into it.

Until you decide to get engaged, your new date needs to fit into your life, not the reverse. If you ultimately break up, your life goes on. If you break up and have commingled everything with this other person, you will think of him or her every time you do anything, and you risk terrible loneliness as well as longer healing time from the breakup.

Once you become engaged, renegotiate the time you spend together and how that is going to look for both of you. You might now go skydiving together in both your former groups but maintain your own skydiving group just for you. This is the time to restructure your leisure time with everyone to accommodate the change in your life. If you decide to only skydive with your spouse, you need to get some new, healthy independent interests on your own. Maintaining this through your life together will keep you healthy, interesting, and safe within proper boundaries, and it will give you the ability to survive if you are ever left alone in life.

> "When you choose your friends, don't be short-changed by choosing personality over character."
> W. Somerset Maugham

The saddest thing to see is an elderly person who did not know what it was like to be alone, or do anything without his or her mate. The healthiest people still live life after a spouse passes away and can do so without guilt. There is no romance to withering away and dying if your spouse dies or if you end up in a divorce. This not only takes a toll on you but on your extended family and friends as well.

Finally, communicate, communicate, communicate. Let your dates know about your schedule and commitments before you embark on an exclusive relationship. Are you one of those people who goes on a date once and thinks the relationship must be exclusive? If so, you are heading for trouble. Date a person casually for a month or two before making the "exclusive dating commitment." Once you do that, have the conversation about time and interests expectations and come to an agreement. If you stick to these guidelines, you will weed out the people who are not right for you fairly quickly, and if a relationship ends, it will have a better shot at ending on good terms.

The bottom line is that interests are like icing on a cake. Icing makes a cake fun, attractive, and enticing. Interests can do this same thing in a relationship. Similar interests add "commonality" to a relationship, but interests in themselves are rarely enough to hold a relationship together. People with different interests can survive and even thrive in a relationship. However, couples with vastly different interests often become frustrated with each other after a while.

If interests are the icing on the cake, then what is the cake made of? Values—which brings us to the next question.

How Similar Are Our Values?

Values come from our beliefs about right and wrong as well as our sense of morality. Values are convictions. Whereas interests are likened to "those things we enjoy doing," values are "those things we believe and must do." Values also largely determine our direction and purpose in life and strike at the core of who we are. Values are much more difficult to change than interests. While there's some room for compromise, significant alterations change who we are.

Your interest may be dancing, but your values will determine if you're dancing with a ballet company at Rockefeller Center in New York or pole dancing in the seedy part of your hometown. Your interest may be in becoming a lawyer, but, again, your values will determine if you're an honest lawyer or a crooked one.

Sharing similar values is extremely important in a long-term relationship, much more so than similar interests. A survey of some singles groups as well as some groups of married couples identified what values they felt were most important for two people planning a lifetime commitment to hold in common. Here are some of their thoughts.

Money

What are your beliefs about money? We're not talking about wealth here, but rather, money in general. How important is it to you? How important should it be to your partner? Obviously, people need money to live, but what other things in life are more important to you than money? What would you sacrifice for money—your reputation, your integrity?

Do you know how your partner would answer these questions? These may seem like odd questions, but both singles and married couples reminded us how vital it is to share similar values with a partner about money. The partner who believes in thriftiness and the need to save for a rainy day will soon become frustrated with a person who spends money like it's burning a hole in his pocket. One woman said she lost her marriage due to opposing values concerning money.

> "If you want things to be different, perhaps the answer is to become different yourself."
> NORMAN VINCENT PEALE

Her husband made good money from his job, but they were continually broke because every time he got a paycheck, he gambled it away. He seriously believed that he would hit it big one day in his betting and they would be set for life. His wife realized that even if he did hit it big, he would then turn around and gamble that away too, trying to win an even bigger jackpot.

How does a frugal, yet generous, person deal with a partner who's downright cheap and miserly? One couple faced this very dilemma and, sadly, their marriage ended in divorce. The wife was generous, while her husband held on tightly to every dollar he made. He wouldn't allow the family to turn on the home air conditioner until July 4th, no matter how hot the weather got. If he thought his wife put too much money in the offering at church, he would take some of the money right out of the offering plate. Not wanting to face this embarrassing situation anymore, his wife started mailing donation checks to their church. Her husband, however, was one step ahead and would call the bank to stop payment on the checks. You may think the husband was just trying to be cautious with their money so they could make ends meet, but the irony of the story is that they were wealthy. The couple remained embattled in nasty divorce disputes for over a year. The wife had become bitter and made several statements that her goal in the divorce was to cost him as much money as possible.

Money is one of the most common issues over which couples fight. Having similar values about money does not mean you'll never have a disagreement about finances. It will, however, provide a common ground and lessen the negative impact that money issues can have on the relationship.

Wealth and Status

How important is being wealthy to you? What is your idea of being wealthy? If you had a million dollars, what would you do with it? Would your partner's answers be similar to yours? Why do so many couples split up after winning a multi-million-dollar lottery? Because they have different values when it comes to wealth.

How important is status to you? Do you know people who live in large houses, drive the latest sports cars, and drink expensive wines at the country club, while they live in debt up to their eyeballs? Do you know other people who live in modest homes and drive station wagons, yet have millions in the bank? Resist the temptation to make a judgment of whether these scenarios are right or wrong. What matters most is that you and your partner are both on the same end of the spectrum.

Many couples never compare their values concerning money, wealth, status, prestige, power, and so forth before they are actually married. Why is this? Much of the reason lies in the fact that most dating couples marry before they actually achieve wealth, status, or power. The average age for a first marriage in this country today is the midtwenties. It can be difficult to discuss feelings and beliefs about something you've never experienced on your own. It can also appear presumptuous to plan how you will deal with wealth and status before you actually achieve them.

You can determine a great deal about people's beliefs by closely observing how they live with what they have presently. Do they seem content? How materialistic are they? How concerned are they about impressing others? Do they stretch the truth to impress others? Do they use people to achieve status? Cluing in on today's behaviors will give you a good glimpse into tomorrow's behaviors. Nancy's story is a good example.

Nancy was a resident physician who began dating Ron, a handsome pharmaceutical salesman, shortly after they met at a medical conference. Nancy was mesmerized by the attention Ron lavished on her with expensive dinners, gifts, and romantic limo rides. Ron claimed that as the company's top marketing representative in the country, he was highly paid.

One afternoon a top executive from Ron's company stopped by Nancy's clinic and, after ensuring complete confidentiality, divulged that Ron was being investigated for fraud. Not only did he expense their dates and list them as "sales calls," but he also had bogus signatures of numerous other physicians in the city who had supposedly accompanied him on these outings.

Nancy was angry and heartbroken as she realized that Ron had duped her into thinking he was a highly paid, top sales representative for this pharmaceutical company, when he was actually a con man. These wonderful romantic evenings they shared—which he said were worth every penny he spent—were actually free for him. Ron not only lost his job that day but his girlfriend as well when he tried to put status before integrity.

Occupation/Work

Understand that as people grow in their jobs, their interests and ideas about wealth, status, and finances can change. You might see someone who appears to value wealth and status, but in reality the big house and nice car are not the key issue. When you get down to the real issue, the house and car are merely a manifestation of something deeper—motivation and drive. Sometimes people can be accused of being materialistic when they are not materialistic at all.

Look at your own occupation and map out where you want to see yourself in 5, 10, 15, and 20 years. Does that include further education, promotions, starting your own busi-

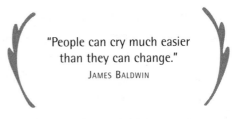

"People can cry much easier than they can change."
JAMES BALDWIN

ness, and the like? Or do you simply want to go to work, earn a paycheck, and come home? Do you easily stagnate without growth and improvement, or would you enjoy just doing the same job for the next 20 years? Remember this as you search for a mate. Look for a person who feels the same way you do in this area.

This is important because even though you and your partner are in two different places from eight to five daily, your careers are still impacted by each other. Someone who wants to go to work, earn a paycheck, and do the same job until retirement may not always sympathize with what you need to do as a person of growth. Jealousy may enter in. If you are a person of growth, you may experience great frustration if you marry someone without occupational drive.

Some couples agree to work as a team for the overall success of the family. A career woman recently married a career man, both in their thirties. Her dream had always been to give up her work and be a wife and mother, supporting her husband from the home. This was exactly what her husband wanted because his job was very demanding. During their courtship they decided she would never work again, unless she wanted to. In this case, the decision was made for the partnership, and the differences in work/occupation actually served the relationship instead of eroding it. As long as you view your efforts as a team, you'll hold the key to overcoming occupational differences.

Family and Friends

How do you view the relationships you'll have with family and friends *after* you are married? This must be discussed and agreed upon during dating. As long as you make your decisions during your dating phase, you can present a united front to everyone. Waiting until after marriage could cause serious resentment in one or both of you, as well as your extended family and friends. Often premarital counselors will have couples map out their time and activities with extended relationships, going so far as to schedule the ways birthdays and holidays will be celebrated. The time and energy you spend with loved ones in the extended family circle also encompasses telephone time. Begin to observe these guidelines during your engagement, and make sure you tell your extended relations what you are doing and why. If you communicate clearly, and demonstrate you are not cutting them out of your lives but making an investment in your new married life, friends and family ought to support you.

Service to Others

Discuss with your partner how important service to others is to each of you. Some people have never lifted a finger to help anyone else, and they don't understand altruism. They are not necessarily selfish; they were just not brought up to understand the concept of serving others.

Agreeing on what service to others will look like will greatly enhance your married life and is just as important as planning your time with family and friends. It would be great to help the disadvantaged every night and on weekends, but that would come at the expense of your relationship. Remember that no matter how much good you do, you still need a healthy balance for this area to be an enhancement rather than a distraction to your relationship.

Religious Beliefs

Religious beliefs are certainly values that determine much of who we are. Altering these would mean changing one's very core. Our surveys showed that having similar religious beliefs was an important factor to most people who are in the process of choosing a mate.

Even people who ranked spirituality as a low priority in their lives were actually attracted to others who possessed firm spiritual beliefs. Those who ranked spirituality as a high priority in their own lives felt strongly about finding a mate who shared similar religious values. It was also important to them to marry someone from their same faith.

We asked the question, particularly of those who identified themselves as Christians, how important it was to marry someone in their particular denomination (Catholic, Baptist, Pentecostal, etc.). The majority felt that interdenominational marrying was acceptable. They agreed that the more similar the denominations were, particularly in theology and styles of worship, the easier it would be to adjust to this difference. For instance, an Episcopalian marrying a Catholic would require less of an adjustment than would a marriage between a Catholic and a Pentecostal.

Many people told us they would be willing to change denominations in order to make a relationship work. We spoke with several pastors from nondenominational churches who confirmed that each year they see newly married couples from separate denominations join their congregations. Some of

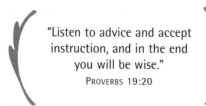

"Listen to advice and accept instruction, and in the end you will be wise."
PROVERBS 19:20

the pastors thought the increase in popularity of nondenominational churches over the last few decades has provided a new choice for interdenominational couples who once would have had to choose which spouse's church they would attend.

Another pastor of a large denominational church shared with us that he felt the trend among today's younger generation is to choose the church based on a smorgasbord of offerings, with the denominational affiliation as a secondary factor. Churches are chosen because of what they offer (active singles department, style of worship, the pastor and his approach to teaching). Because of this, some young people have no problem transferring to a church of another denomination if they feel that church better meets their needs.

According to pastors interviewed, the key issue isn't marriage within different denominations, but rather the problems that arise when two people marry with different levels of commitment to their faith. Two people raised not only in the same denomination but also in the same hometown church can still be on separate spiritual levels. When this happens in a marriage, the relational harmony may be undermined. Moral convictions, issues related to church (such as how often we'll go, how involved we'll be), and issues such as tithing are strongly affected by what the pastors referred to as one's "maturity of faith."

Large differences in maturity of faith within a married couple can be a constant source of conflict in a relationship. One pastor recalled a couple who came to him for counseling because the husband felt his wife was cheating on their income taxes. She had not reported several thousand dollars of income that had been paid in cash for odd jobs the previous year. She felt there was nothing wrong with this practice and refused to divulge how much she had received in cash payments. In the end the pair agreed to file their taxes separately rather than jointly.

We had the opportunity to visit with many marriage and family counselors concerning the issue of interfaith marriages. Overwhelmingly, they agreed that the biggest problems in these marriages concern dealing with in-laws and deciding how to handle religious matters when children arrive.

Couples from separate faiths often find that just because they can work out these differences with their partners doesn't mean that each of their respective families can. The counselors gave numerous examples of spouses who weren't accepted by their in-laws because of their religious affiliation. Holidays were particularly difficult for couples estranged from family members.

The problem only worsened when children came along. Children's names, for instance, are heavily influenced by the religious affiliation of their families. Muslim boys often carry popular Islamic names like Muhammad and Abdul, whereas Jewish names would come from the Old Testament—Abraham and David, for example. Not only can there be pressure on the parents about naming the children, but there can also be extreme pressure put on the children as to which religion they will embrace.

Alex, an eighteen-year-old high-school graduate, had a Muslim father and a Christian mother. Alex told us he had always been confused when it came to religion. Even though his parents had never tried to force him to believe a certain way, Alex still felt that by choosing one faith he would disappoint the parent practicing the other faith. Alex decided that he was going to practice Islam, largely because he saw his father being more devout in his faith than his mother. Alex also said that he would never marry a non-Muslim. "It might have worked out okay for my parents to disagree about their faiths, but it was a poor choice for my sister and me. I still love them, but I would never do to my kids what they did to me," was Alex's conclusion.

Dating someone with the notion that you will convert him or her to your faith is also unwise. This is widely known in Christian counseling circles as "missionary dating." Experienced Christian counselors will assure you that missionary dating often does not turn out well. It also raises the question, "If someone converts to a new faith in order to remain in a romantic relationship, did he or she really make a heartfelt decision?"

The bottom line is that faith should be a common ground that brings two people closer rather than acting as an obstacle to intimacy. Many couples acknowledge their faith similarities and differences before they marry but never grasp the impact those differences will have on their relationship. Remember that it's not being different that dooms a relationship but it's the extent of those differences.

How can we know if our values are similar? The only way to truly know someone's values is to spend time with that person. By "time" I don't mean 24 hours a day for two weeks straight, but shorter time periods over a span of months. See how the other person treats you. How does that person's behavior in times of stress differ from behavior in times of success? Those people who are genuine will stand the test of time. Those people who are deceivers will be exposed by time. This truth should make you wonder about and question anyone who insists on rushing a relationship.

You can discover more about people's values by watching what they do than by listening to what they say. The phrase "I can't hear what you're saying because your actions are too loud" applies here. None of us is 100 percent the person we claim to be (and think we are as well). That's just a fact of being human. But some people are close to being zero percent of the persons they claim to be.

Single and married people alike told us that integrity is a huge issue when it comes to choosing a marriage partner. What constitutes integrity in a relationship? It basically comes down to this: Are you who you say you are? Do your actions match your words? Do your behaviors support your proclaimed values?

Marriage partners get to see each other during both the worst and best times. That's why it's important for you to know the person you marry so well that you observe him or her in a variety of situations and times of stress. Traditional marriage vows ask both the bride and groom to promise to take care of each other in good times and bad, in sickness and health. We hope that when your wedding day arrives, you both know how the other handles stress.

Do Our Personality Types Mesh?

Do similar personalities get along best or do opposite personalities do the best together? Fortunately, your personality type does not necessarily determine with whom you are compatible. There are great relationships between every possible combination of personality type; there are also horrible relationships between every combination of personality type.

Most of us, however, tend to prefer certain personality traits. You may like soft-spoken, conservative guys who are secure with themselves. This does not mean the first man you meet who fits this description will be the guy of your dreams. Personality types are better used as a guideline to sort out which people we are most likely to stick with and which are most likely to wear us out.

Finding immediate attraction to someone with your same personality type is easy. It is refreshing to believe, *Hey, somebody finally understands me.* But the wonderful and the wicked often come together. The exact traits that draw us to each other can also drive us crazy. You may love your boyfriend's free spirit and spontaneity. However, when he spontaneously decides to shave his hair into a Mohawk, his spontaneity now totally frustrates you.

Another factor to be aware of is that under stress people's personalities can be radically different from when life is going well. A

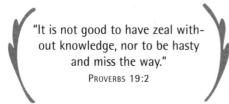

"It is not good to have zeal without knowledge, nor to be hasty and miss the way."
PROVERBS 19:2

person's basic personality is largely set, but his or her day-to-day personality can change based on the day's events. Also, we act differently around different people. Do you act the same around a person of romantic interest as you do around your grandmother? Another variable is that we behave differently in different situations. You might handle situations much differently during the time of day when you are most energetic as opposed to when you are worn out.

So how do you find out your partner's other "personalities"? By experiencing life in different situations; that's the only way to really know. Instead of doing that, some people try to use those widely available Internet personality tests. The problem with using free tests on the Internet to determine the compatibility of potential partners is that these tests measure personality under ideal circumstances— not real life. They only measure what *you* think your personality is like—how you see yourself, rather than how others see you. Those tests are also largely "state-based," which means that they are based on your thoughts and feelings for that day. Your results could actually change in five minutes. Many people have a pretty accurate sense of their personalities, but just as many people have poor insight about how others see them.

Personality tests also make assumptions about you based on broad concepts. Here's what happens as you take a personality test, for example. The first question asks you to rate how energetic you are on a scale of 1–5. Well, compared to what? You're a 4 or 5 (high energy) compared to your grandmother, but perhaps you're a 1 (low energy) compared to your dog. Your energy levels fluctuate and so will your answer, depending on the time of the day, the time of the month, and how much you idealize being energetic. If you consider it a positive trait, you'll probably give yourself a higher score. Say you select a 4. If you select any lower, the Internet dating service may fix you up with a couch potato who wants to watch football all day. If you put a 5, they may pair you up with a hyperactive guy— and those types will usually end up getting on your last good nerve.

Do Men and Women Think Differently?

The drive to bond with someone of the opposite sex is natural, healthy, and powerful. Many people say they never felt whole until they finally found that person to share life with. Females are often attracted by traits of maleness—protection, strength, loving firmness, etc. Males are equally attracted by female traits—nurturance, tenderness, respect, etc. Remember "that list" which we all carry around in our heads? Well, a female's list will differ from a male's list.

Women and men must remember that their brains are different from each other's. A woman should not expect a man to act like a girlfriend. Though a woman may say she wants a sensitive man, the minute he becomes a girlie-man, she will likely be turned off. A man will often listen and share, but only after he's finished his projects for the day. The middle of a football game is not the best time to try to have a heart-to-heart discussion.

A man should ensure that he has not scheduled too many must-do things when with his partner, so that he'll have time in case an issue comes up that must be addressed. He shouldn't ignore a girl-friend's attempt to connect during the day and then expect to have a romantic date with her later that evening. Hearing and validating his girlfriend's feelings will get him much closer to that romantic evening. Both genders must respect each other's differences.

One last bit of caution to be aware of about "that list" before we proceed: Having a list is good, but don't make it too tight unless you are willing to do *your* part to help it happen. A good example of this is Seema, a late-20-something Indian female who had "that list." She always dated quality guys, but they generally had one fatal flaw, at least in terms of being a match for her. She wanted a guy from her Indian culture, but due to the fact that Indians are a tight-knit community, she already knew there were no candidates for her from this group in her city. So Seema felt compelled to leave the midsized city where she was raised for the purpose of finding a guy who fit her list.

Seema moved to a larger city and began the task of meeting new friends. This was extremely traumatic for her, but it was necessary for her future happiness. She ultimately found the perfect guy *for her*. She was 34 years old before she married, but she says she is extremely thankful she stuck to her guns and waited for Mr. Right. Would she tell you she wishes she had married earlier? Yes and no. She says it would have been nice to marry slightly earlier, but had she settled on someone who was not a good fit, she realizes she would be unhappy. Seema was realistic, and she did it right.

❡

Reality Check

In what ways does your "list" fit where you are living?

In what ways does your "list" not fit where you are living?

Name three ways you will find dating partners that fit your criteria based on your part of the equation. (Where will you meet them? Who will you enlist to help?)

What are you willing to do to make a match with a person who more closely meets your needs? (Examples include: join an organization where these people congregate, take a class to increase your knowledge base, and so forth.)

Write It Down

List your top three personal interests. Have your dating partner list his or hers.

List your three most important personal values. Have your dating partner list his or hers.

How would you describe your personality? Have your dating partner describe his or hers.

What interests, values, and personality traits do you admire or value in a potential mate? Have your dating partner list his or hers.

Do you have what it takes to find a person meeting your criteria?

Issues to consider:

• Do you live in a city where you can find this person?

• Do you have sufficient contact with people who run in the circles of the mate you wish to find? If not, where will you start finding those contacts?

• Do you have viable attributes to attract the person on your list—comparable in education, occupation, etc.? If not, how will you grow in order to be compatible with your "wish list" mate?

(5)

Proceed with Caution

Singles say…

> …most people cannot be trusted at first.
>
> …they will consider having sex even if they are not in love.
>
> …family opinion of a partner is important, but also admit holding on to relationships too long just to spite family or friends.

So you met that person who captured your attention, and you've been going out for two weeks. In fact, this person seems to be a perfect fit! Why not go ahead and get married? After all, the vibes are good—and people have always affirmed your great intuition.

Well, relationships are much more complex than this. It is impossible to know another person completely in two weeks unless there's not much there to know. Healthy relationships take time to build and are often like expensive cheese, which tastes better with age. Every one of us has idiosyncrasies, likes and dislikes, and even quirky habits. People are not simple. The old saying that "Rome wasn't built in a day" is also true about building a solid, lasting relationship.

Impulsively marrying someone after a brief courtship is a lot like playing *Let's Make a Deal,* that famous game show of the seventies. In the show, a contestant was presented with a choice of three doors. Behind one door was a worthless prize, another concealed a mediocre gift, and the third hid a fantastic prize. You could see the outsides of the doors, but that gave no clue to what was behind them. You chose blindly.

The dating relationship is your chance to see behind the door before making your final choice. Use it wisely. Taking shortcuts may get you there faster, but you may end up disappointed.

LET'S TALK

One question singles frequently ask is, "How should a relationship progress?" Relationships usually start out with "small talk" and slowly progress to self-disclosure. Disclosure is when you reveal something about yourself that most people don't know. Many people start with safe disclosures, which are things you wouldn't want everyone in the world to know, but you wouldn't necessarily be crushed if someone found out about them. For instance, you might talk about reasons for a past breakup or give your personal opinion about someone else.

Safe disclosures allow you to test the trustworthiness of another person. This can be anxiety provoking as you wonder: *Will he gossip to others about what I said? Will he talk to me again? Will he keep this to himself? Will he laugh at me and never call me again?* The best advice for making disclosures is to proceed thoughtfully and carefully; starting with safe subjects is the wisest route. You will find many nice people who have problems keeping confidential information confidential. If you realize you might be dating one of these people, proceed with caution and remember the old saying: Fool me once, shame on you. Fool me twice, shame on me.

> "If you want to know your past—look into your present conditions. If you want to know your future—look into your present actions."
> CHINESE PROVERB

Many of us secretly fear some level of rejection and hesitate to allow others to see our real desires and needs largely for this reason. You have to do a real balancing act here. If you don't share personal needs and desires, then the relationship stays on a superficial level, but sharing too much can be damaging as well. Don't worry; you can master this. One rule of thumb is discerning beforehand what you feel comfortable sharing and not just deciding in the heat of the moment what will be disclosed.

Once trustworthiness has been established with *safe disclosure*, you can begin *self-disclosure*. This is where you can freely talk about yourself, issues of your life, and your views. Deep bonding begins here as self-disclosure places you in the position of vulnerability. Self-disclosure is not about airing your dirty laundry, such as how your "ex" is a horrible person, but rather communicating how you feel about today's issues: "I'm afraid my boss doesn't like me." "It bothers me when you don't call for two days."

As time progresses, relationships move into the discovery-disclosure phase, which marks the sign of a truly intimate relationship. This happens when both partners have the freedom to acknowledge or even point out bothersome behaviors and attitudes in each other. Each partner accepts this because he or she knows the other partner has his or her best interests in mind. When couples use self-disclosure correctly, it strengthens their individual characters and their joint character. Two spirits prove wiser than one as couples learn to compensate for each other as well. One's weak area could be the other's strength. For this to work, however, both parties have to be honest and sincere and know where the limits of disclosure ought to be.

Karol is in medical school. When she is approached for dates, she makes sure to let prospective suitors know how dedicated she is to her education. Medical school is consuming, and dates are informed that for now Karol will not be able to invest her time in pursuing a serious relationship. She knows that most relationships wither in the shadow of medical school, and she also knows that pursuing a quality relationship would require more time than she can currently invest. Secure men with balanced lives do not have a problem with the boundaries Karol has set for her relationships.

Men who are only attracted to surface appearances and who want to be number one in her life will soon fall by the wayside. Things won't always be this way for Karol, but she knows that it will take a self-assured, confident man to ultimately be her partner. As you might imagine, taking longer to get to know men at a slower pace also helps Karol understand the kind of men she is dating. She has had men throw fits after a couple of dates, stating, "You didn't call me back. Are you mad at me?" These men obviously were not listening when Karol explained the rigors of her daily life, or they just cared more about their own desires.

Karol also keeps her disclosures at a healthy level. Discussing family, friends, pets, goals, and dreams is fine with her, but even if she really likes a dating partner, she is careful not to lead him on. Of course, sex is definitely out, not just because of her moral standards, but also because she would not want her dates to believe the relationship to be more intimate than it truly is.

Karol is fortunate. Her pursuit of medical school actually helps weed out anyone who cannot understand this type of lifestyle, while also allowing her to get to know people slowly without the overwhelming blindness that sudden romance can bring. Clear vision during the first part of dating is paramount to future success. Karol is not likely to be blinded by feelings, overlooking potential red flags that could signal trouble for the future. Romantic feelings are wonderful, but cultivated slowly, they allow for more success than whirlwind courtships.

Men often experience difficulty mastering the more intimate phase of the relationship. Males are often reared to express as little emotion as possible (keep a poker face) and to hide areas of vulnerability. Men usually have a more active left side of the brain (parietal lobe) than their female counterparts. This part of the brain functions in problem solving, memory, and position sense. You need your left parietal lobe to remember how to perform tasks.

Most women possess increased activity in the right side of their brains compared to men. This side is more involved in reading social cues, having religious experiences, and identifying signals from their own bodies.

Men are often considered task oriented, while women are seen as more relationship ori- ented. A man's communi- cation often focuses on problem solving—getting from point A to point B. Emotional bonding com- prises a larger part of female conversations. Most men don't call other men on the phone just to see how they are feeling. Men call because they need some- thing, and once the transaction is done, they hang up.

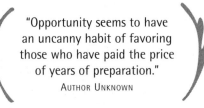

"Opportunity seems to have an uncanny habit of favoring those who have paid the price of years of preparation."
AUTHOR UNKNOWN

Generally, women want to talk to their romantic partners about their feelings, but men just want to solve the problem at hand. Prob- lem solving is great, but for many women the purpose of the con- versation is validation of feelings.

In marriage counseling, therapists witness numerous instances in which the husband has no clue there is anything wrong in the marriage. This probably explains why it is the wife who seeks mar- riage counseling most of the time.

That was the situation for John. He sat stunned as his wife, Jacqui, cried her eyes out during their first session of marriage counseling, indicating the past 12 years had been "miserable." John said he had no clue his wife had even been unhappy. Jacqui claimed she told her husband repeatedly that she was not happy in their marriage, but he never "heard" her. Marital therapists will tell you this scenario is not uncommon. There are always two sides to these heartbreaking marriage stories. John was not there emotionally for Jacqui and had no clue about how off-base he was. In John's defense, however, emotional support had never been part of the relationship—no wonder he was stunned.

"After three days they found him in the temple courts, sitting among the teachers, listening to them and asking them questions."
LUKE 2:46

A detailed history of their relationship would reveal the two had never developed emotional bonding while dating. When asked why she married a man who didn't understand her feelings (which seemed important to her), Jacqui admitted she thought it would happen once they were married. The lesson here is not to wait until you have been unhappily married for years to address a problem. That is what dating is for.

Now John says he has learned a hard lesson but one that is worthwhile, though he now is single again. He takes responsibility for not nurturing Jacqui, but also realizes he needs to ask more questions so he can be the kind of mate a partner needs.

BUILDING TRUST

We've established that talking at ever-deeper levels moves a relationship forward. The goal is not to just talk, but to develop mutual trust, an essential element of any committed relationship. It would be great if people were 100 percent faithful and trustworthy. Unfortunately, none of us reaches that standard. Most people are not looking for perfection, but instead are searching for the qualities of trust-worthiness and faithfulness in the people they date.

Just as you are testing your partner's trustworthiness, yours is on the line as well. Let's look at behaviors that can interfere with building mutual trust.

Violating Confidentiality

For someone to reveal very personal information to you is a great privilege. Never undermine your trustworthiness by repeating that confidential information to anyone. Doing so could ruin your reputation and break another's heart.

One-Sided Disclosure

We've all met people who will tell you their life stories in the first hour of your acquaintance. They indiscriminately discuss their family issues, sexual problems, and career dreams before mutual trust has been established. Beware of people who are too friendly too fast. They are usually emotionally insecure, shallow, or immature. Also, be discreet in what you disclose about yourself to this type of person. They have no problem sharing your personal information with the next person they meet. Nor do they have any hesitation about repeating what you say about someone else. They're not trying to be vindictive or cause trouble; they just don't use good judgment in social situations.

Secrecy

Someone who is very secretive should alert your warning radar. These people let you in on few details of their lives. They are often vague when asked about their jobs, families, and even past or present relationships. In real life most women would soon tire of any long-term relationship with this James Bond type. His life is secretive; you can't call him to see how his day is going. He's got an agenda that you're not a part of.

Lying

It may seem obvious that nothing undermines trust like lying. But since we're all human and prone to lie, be careful not to fudge the truth even about small matters, because once a person perceives that you lie, it is very difficult to restore trust. We'll talk much more about this important obstacle to trust in the next chapter.

Develop Healthy Commitment

Relationship commitment usually only begins once a certain level of trust is established. Two forms of commitment described by Scott M. Stanley in his book *The Power of Commitment* are dedication commitment and constraint commitment. Dedication commitment conveys an internal state of devotion to a person, while constraint commitment indicates a sense of obligation.

As you can imagine, dedication commitment can develop a powerful emotional connection, as the couple feels safe enough to begin divulging their insecurities and even their deepest hurts. Feeling that someone of the opposite sex understands and accepts you can be exhilarating; however, it is still wise to proceed with cautious restraint when sharing your innermost thoughts.

People who have constraint commitment toward a partner are generally less happy and content than those who have dedication commitment. You can imagine that a feeling of obligation to someone does not help develop strong positive emotional feelings. Sometimes obligating factors, such as a pregnancy before marriage, can cause constraint commitment to dominate a relationship. A boyfriend who discloses too much too soon may evoke feelings of guilt in his girlfriend to the point she thinks, *I can't break up with him because he trusts me completely; I would hurt him too much.*

Keep in mind that constraint commitment is not an issue you should have to address in a dating relationship. If you are feeling obligation toward a dating partner, you should examine your feelings and consider getting out of the relationship.

The Destructive Power of Sex

Starting sexual relations is tempting to many at this stage of the relationship, where mutual trust and commitment have been established. But beware of its potential destructiveness. Sex is natural and created by God to be enjoyable—in the context of marriage. Fire, when used properly, can cook food, give heat,

"Discretion will protect you, and understanding will guard you."
Proverbs 2:11

and provide light, but this same wonderful gift can also injure, kill, and destroy when used in the wrong place or at the wrong time. In the same way, sex is two-sided. Sex is very powerful and can be used to celebrate intimacy and create new life, bonding a married couple together. It can also injure people both emotionally and physically when it occurs outside the boundaries of marriage.

Some couples use sex in an attempt to enhance a relationship. The problem is that it acts more like dynamite and can destroy the bond you've been developing. Many people have sex and intimacy confused. They are not the same. Sex is only one part of intimacy. Sex also doesn't create intimacy but is a culmination of intimacy in marriage. Sex never makes a bad relationship better; it just makes you forget the real problems for a while. It does not fix broken relationships either.

Sexual activity in the early stages of a relationship creates a false sense of closeness, which can lead to heartache later when one partner discovers the level of commitment is not what he or she assumed it was. Counselors see destructive patterns emerge again and again in sexually active dating couples. The couple starts spending much of their time together having sex or getting ready to. Even if they go out on a date, their minds are anticipating the end of the evening. Communication between the two stagnates for a while then often begins to crumble. For the partner who thought the relationship was more serious, betrayal and humiliation are often the result.

FAMILY AND FRIENDS

As your relationship moves forward, meet your partner's family and friends, and you'll begin to envision your future. Does your partner's family resemble yours in terms of values and beliefs? Do you get along with your partner's friends, and do they have values similar to yours? If you see dramatic differences in your date's family and friends, you can probably count on problems down the road. If these people are different from you and your significant other, a long period of dating will help you determine if your significant other will likely return to the habits and behaviors of his family of origin. It is possible for a person to break free from a dysfunctional family, and you should expect that person to have broken free and changed prior to meeting you. All people want to be better, but is your partner looking to you excessively to help him or her stay on course?

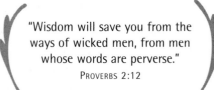

"Wisdom will save you from the ways of wicked men, from men whose words are perverse."
PROVERBS 2:12

Friends can provide a good gauge of what you can expect down the road as well. Does your girlfriend hang out with emotionally immature women who call her day and night? Does your boyfriend binge drink every weekend with the guys? Do not expect this to change. What you are looking at now is likely what you will see in six months, a year, and on into a marriage.

Ignoring these principles can lead to the kind of situation that overwhelmed a young man named Tad.

When Tad began dating Tiffany, he thought she was sweet, quiet, and loving. In the past, Tad had gravitated toward needy women and attempted to rescue each one. Tiffany did not appear to need rescuing, at least at first.

Tad's family knew Tiffany's family. From day one, his family, including his grandparents, warned him that the erratic and extremely detrimental behavior of Tiffany's mother and the dysfunctional nature of their home life could not have escaped visiting itself upon Tiffany in some way. Tad refused to listen to their wise counsel, stating that Tiffany was most like her father, who appeared to have core values similar to Tad's.

Tad's family insisted there must be something wrong with the seemingly perfect father who allowed immorality and chaos to go on within the home. Over time, Tad began to see the real sickness within the family. Rather than distancing himself from Tiffany, he tried to help her, and her family—at the expense of his own education and career.

Eventually Tiffany portrayed herself as a victim to everyone, and Tad's family cautioned him that at some point, she would begin making Tad the bad guy. This began to occur, and Tiffany's behavior became more and more erratic. She began smoking, drinking, and engaging in self-destructive behaviors, as well as constantly accusing Tad of cheating on her. Ultimately, he learned Tiffany had cheated on him. Tad learned a lesson, but only after much loss in his life in terms of education, career, and family bonds.

Looking back, he told his therapist that the only reason he did not listen to his family was because he thought he knew better. He stated that, in the future if everyone told him a date looked, sounded, and acted like a duck, it would be worth considering that he might be dating a duck!

Beware Overexposure

We've discussed disclosure, behavior, trust, commitment, sex, and family and friends as elements in a forward-moving relationship. A word of caution about friendships and dating relationships in this era: With enhanced communication including cell phones and Internet sites comes lack of privacy—potentially for you.

> "A gossip betrays a confidence; so avoid a man who talks too much."
> Proverbs 20:19

Twenty years ago people could date and, unless they burned up the phone lines, keep their interpersonal relationships relatively private. Today, make one wrong move— either real or perceived—and your friend or dating partner could hit the Internet or begin calling and texting everyone she knows to work out the trauma she believes you have caused. This is a huge red flag. Working out problems on the Internet for the world to see or texting everyone on the list eliminates normal opportunities for two people to privately work out their issues.

Suddenly, you may have a world of people who not only know your business and judge you (either fairly or unfairly) but also attempt to jump in and give their two cents' worth. This input may or may not include anything that would help you and your partner. Additionally, people become much braver hiding behind the Internet and text messaging, though their words are exposed for all to read. If you begin checking the home page of someone you're dating and see things that concern you, or if you receive e-mails or text messages that seem out of character for your partner, do not dismiss them. People do crazy things for fun, but if they think or act on the Internet or cell phones in a way that gives you reason to pause, take heed. Behavior that comes out on the Internet or through text messaging will likely pop up in "real life."

A dating relationship usually needs at least several months before you're ready to move on to the next stage, which is considering engagement. These first months should be fun, exciting, and adventurous! If a dating relationship is full of arguments, unhappiness, and drama, it is not the kind of relationship that will prove to be stable for a happy marriage. Many married couples have cherished memories from their early dating days. I hope you will feel the same.

Reality Check

Think about your dating partners up until now.

How does each section in this chapter reflect the journeys of those relationships from your past?

Write It Down

Which dating partners worked through the stages of disclosure discussed at the beginning of the chapter?

Do you follow the stages of disclosure, or do you move too quickly or too slowly?

How has that affected your relationships?

In which relationships have you felt constraint commitment, and why?

Document any failed relationships where family and friends had differing values, beliefs, or behaviors from you. Do you see a pattern?

(6)

Dealing with Problem Areas

Singles say…

> …they are much more likely to consider living together before marriage than they would have been five years ago, even though they believe it is wrong.
>
> …men are perceived to have an easier time getting dates than women.
>
> …they have dated someone who attempted to emotionally, mentally, or verbally abuse them.

You are several months into your dating relationship. As the relationship progresses, a decision concerning exclusivity needs to be made. The agreement of exclusivity should be discussed and boundaries made clear to each person. Be careful not to assume your partner thinks as you do. Clear, open communication will save you heartache if you plainly agree you are exclusive, as well as what that means to each of you.

The key to this stage of the dating relationship is commitment. Both of you are further testing each other's trustworthiness, especially concerning how well your partner's actions match his or her words and promises. Whereas emotional commitment was the key factor in the early days (can I trust you with my emotions?), the relationship now focuses on contractual commitment (can I trust you to do what you say?). In other words, will you keep your promises? Do your actions match your words?

At this point, not only do other people view you as a couple, but you start thinking as a couple as well. You are able to recognize and discuss strengths and weaknesses in each other's character. You can see a clearer, more balanced view of the relationship including the good and the bad aspects. With this increased intimacy and maturity comes a desire to actively work on areas of your relationship that need it. This is a concept expressed in the Serenity Prayer: improving what you can, learning to live with what you can't, and knowing the difference between the two. This is a time of action more than reflection.

BUILD A SOLID FOUNDATION OF TRUST

As you and your partner commit to work through problem areas in your relationship, it is imperative to have a solid level of trust already in place. Honesty is the main ingredient in building trust. If that's correct, then what is the number one factor that destroys trust? Dishonesty, or lying. It doesn't matter how big or small the lies are. In Luke 16:10 we are reminded, "Whoever can be trusted with very little can also be trusted with much, and whoever is dishonest with very little will also be dishonest with much."

Mark Twain called lying "man's most universal weakness." Everybody tells a lie sometime during his or her life. "Have you ever told a lie?" is a common question asked on psychological tests. Psychologists do not really want to know what you've done in the past, but rather whether you are being truthful now. People who answer no to that question are most likely trying to make themselves look desirable (better than they actually are) on the test.

People lie for many reasons, but three main reasons are: to impress others, to avoid responsibility, and to get their own way. Let's spend a little time on each.

People lie to impress others. Have you ever seen fireflies light up a spring night with their flashing colors? What is the male firefly's whole motive? To attract a female. Instead of achieving this goal, many male fireflies are eaten by birds and snatched out of the air by humans, who would have never seen them had they not been showing off. Most of us have probably engaged in "fireflying" at sometime in our lives.

Lying to impress can seem harmless. After all, you're not trying to hurt anyone. The problem is that it backfires—it actually hurts the person telling the lie. When the person you were trying to impress realizes your lack of truthfulness, you look silly. Now everything you tell that person will be suspect.

> "There is a time for departure even when there's no certain place to go."
>
> TENNESSEE WILLIAMS

This type of lie often has some truth mixed in; it's just stretched or exaggerated. So we rationalize that it's okay to say it. When we take an oath in a court of law, we have to swear to tell "the truth, the whole truth, and nothing but the truth." In other words, don't make up a lie, but also don't leave part of the truth out—a half-truth—and don't add to or exaggerate the truth.

A fireflyer likes to one-up you. If you had to walk five miles in the snow as a child, you can bet the fireflyer had to walk six. If you get a raise of one hundred dollars a month, the next day the fireflyer somehow gets a raise of two hundred dollars. Anything you can do, he has done—but just a little bit better. This kind of person becomes tiresome to be around, especially when you discover what motivates this behavior—a feeling of inferiority. The fireflyer might appear to be the most confident person you've ever met, but if the person removes that mask, he or she will reveal an insecure person who is attempting to be accepted.

A close cousin to lying to impress is lying to flatter. The Bible warns us that "whoever flatters his neighbor is spreading a net for his feet" (Proverbs 29:5). In other words, flattery serves as a trap. We are also cautioned that "a lying tongue hates those it hurts, and a flattering mouth works ruin" (Proverbs 26:28).

What would someone want out of a relationship that would cause him or her to heap flattery on another? Sex, money, love, company, protection—you name it. Who falls for this? Those people who believe the flattery. Just as you need to know when someone is full of himself and trying to impress you, you also need to know when someone is full of baloney and trying to flatter you.

> "Some of us think holding on makes us strong, but sometimes it is letting go."
> HERMANN HESSE

Do you find yourself occasionally stretching the truth in an attempt to impress others or get people to like you? If you really want to impress someone and get him or her to like you, don't talk about yourself. Instead, ask that person questions about himself. Allow him to impress you. At the end of the day, he'll be impressed with you even though you hardly said a word about yourself. Also, be lavish in your real praise, but don't flatter your date. If you don't believe this works, just try it for one month. The results will amaze you.

People lie to avoid responsibility. Children discover this tactic early in life. A child will claim that he never dragged all the toys out of his room, even though no one else has been around. While most children soon learn that these claims get them in trouble, some adults continue to lie to get out of trouble or avoid responsibility.

This type of lie will ruin any intimate relationship and may wreck more marriages and friendships than any other factor.

When caught telling a lie, the fibber has three options: make up another story to get out of the first one, blame her actions on someone else, or feign communication problems—which is still blaming, or else come clean and admit the truth. Sadly, most liars choose from the first two options. When we keep lying in an attempt to avoid responsibility, we only dig ourselves a deeper hole.

A third reason people lie is to get their own way. People who engage in this type of lie are out for one person—themselves. And they don't care who gets trampled in the process. The Bible describes this type of liar: "Truthful lips endure forever, but a lying tongue lasts only a moment" (Proverbs 12:19). A man says, "I love you," in order to persuade a woman to engage in sexual intimacy. A woman says, "I don't feel well; please take me home," when she's simply bored with her date.

While most people lie for the reasons mentioned above, there is a more insidious type of liar—the most serious by far—the pathological liar. The distinguishing mark of this liar is that he lies when the truth would actually fit better. He'll make up a huge story when the real story would have been fine. It's as if he's addicted to lying. Anyone who tries to have a serious relationship with a pathological liar usually ends up deeply confused. This kind of liar can actually make you think you're going crazy. Before you realize you're with a liar, he'll have roped you into a deep relationship, using all the liar's tricks. What usually does pathological liars in, though, is the need to cover their lies with more lies. Pretty soon they can't remember what they have and have not said. When their stories are challenged, they deny what they said, feign confusion, or act like they really didn't mean to say that.

Habitual malignant lying is one sign of a sociopath or antisocial personality disorder. These people may actually appear social and charming, but those who date them describe them as a type of Dr. Jekyll and Mr. Hyde. The person can portray one personality, then almost as if a switch were flipped, he or she becomes a different person.

You can have a relationship with a liar, but it will only be on the surface. It's impossible to trust someone who lies. I'm not talking about one lie here but a continual habit of lying. It doesn't matter how sweet the person is, how good-looking, how nice, or how much fun. Lying ruins trust. Intimacy requires self-disclosure and trust. How can you develop trust in someone when you don't know if what he or she is self-disclosing is the truth?

Foolishness tells you that the person will change. Wisdom tells you to break off your relationship with the liar because he or she has a poor prognosis for changing. She might tell you she'll change, but after she knows she has snagged you, she'll likely revert to lying.

Do you tell false stories or even half-truths to your partner? Do you omit information? Ask yourself why you lie. Have you always lied, or is it a part of this relationship only? If it is part of this relationship, examine the reasons. What are you afraid of? Get to the bottom of this question quickly, and take care of it on your end, before you allow lying to become a part of every aspect of your life. Once you let it into one area, it won't be long before it infiltrates everything.

If your partner is truth-challenged, the problem will not go away without a lot of hard work—but not by you. If you find you are expending energy helping someone else overcome this issue, you are doing too much. Decide at this point, while it is not too late, whether you want to continue in the relationship. The prognosis is not good for these people, despite your hopes for their recovery.

Without trust, there will be little commitment to work through difficult issues. Therefore, the first area you and your partner must tackle is your commitment to be honest with each other.

RELATIONSHIP CANCERS

In his book *The DNA of Relationships,* Gary Smalley likens various types of relationship problems to cancer. Cancer is feared because no one is totally immune from its grip. However, if cancer is diagnosed in its early stages and then treated appropriately, the chances of survival are usually good. What happens if you ignore cancer? Sooner or later it overcomes you.

The same can happen when you treat relationship cancers early. Your relationship becomes healthier. The damaging behaviors and attitudes are removed, allowing you to move forward and grow closer than ever before. Ignoring relationship cancers will destroy the relationship. I'm not saying you'll break up. I've seen couples with horrible untreated relationship cancer go to the altar and make lifetime commitments to each other. You may stay together the rest of your lives, but it will be a sick and anemic marriage relationship until you deal with the cancer head-on.

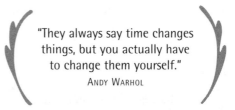

"They always say time changes things, but you actually have to change them yourself."

ANDY WARHOL

So, what exactly are the relationship cancers? They are the attitudes or behaviors exhibited by you and/or your partner that are harmful to the relationship. These attitudes and behaviors diminish love, trust, commitment, and intimacy between you. Studies show what is seen in clinical practices: No amount of love or positive traits can override untreated relationship cancers.

No dating relationship is perfect, and every relationship takes work as it faces its share of struggles. We all exhibit behaviors and attitudes that at times can irritate our mates. That's not what I'm talking about regarding relationship cancers. Relationship cancers are continued maladaptive behaviors that consistently undermine the relationship. Let's examine some common types of relationship cancers.

Poor Conflict Resolution

Most couples have experienced their first argument by the time they reach exclusivity. Some couples are pros at arguing by now and can get downright angry with each other at the slightest provocation. All relationships experience conflict; in fact they're not healthy if they don't. What's important is how you, as a couple, handle the conflict. Do you resolve it? Is this process usually constructive or destructive? If you answered "destructive," then it is imperative that you address the problem before you decide to marry. There must be set boundaries when you settle conflicts, and both of you must know those limits. This will help keep your conflicts constructive, which will help grow the relationship.

If a partner says, "You can't put limits on me and expect me to follow them when I'm mad," then beware. Both men and women seek help with anger-management problems, and many of them report going into destructive rages when angered. They also claim a complete loss of emotional control. Yet these same people often manage to control their anger in public places or the workplace. If a coworker makes them mad, they can't physically touch him or even verbally assault him. Bottom line: If you can control your behavior in public, you should be able to control it in private as well.

> "Failure is the opportunity to begin again, more intelligently."
> HENRY FORD

As imperfect people, we get on each other's nerves and behave in ways that are upsetting. How we deal with these issues in large part sets the tone for the relationship. How we express our anger is a key to building the relationship or demolishing it piece by piece.

Anger is an emotion and does have its place in life. However, it is much like fire—it can be useful, such as in cooking food and warming your house, or it can be destructive when allowed to burn down the house. Anger is the emotional response that leads us to stand up for our sense of conviction and self-worth. It is the method by which we express anger that makes it positive or negative.

Aggressive Anger

Aggressive anger tends to be abrasive, insensitive, and usually accompanied by connotations of judgment. Aggressive anger rarely achieves its desired result, which is resolving the situation. Instead, the problem remains perpetually unresolved, the angry person remains angry, and the other person returns the anger. Examples of aggressive anger are ranting, raving, screaming, cursing, blaming, name calling, temper outbursts, kicking walls or doors, throwing objects, or even physical aggression. Some young men engage in this behavior because they believe it makes them "righteous avengers." Any behavior can be justified for righteousness or avenging a wrong in these people's minds. The person who is the object of this type of anger usually suffers substantially, but in the end the person perpetuating it suffers too as the behavior makes satisfying relationships impossible.

> "Do not make friends with a hot-tempered man, do not associate with one easily angered, or you may learn his ways and get yourself ensnared."
>
> PROVERBS 22:24-25

Sarcasm

Even though sarcasm is not necessarily accompanied by screaming and cursing, it is similar to aggressive anger. Sarcasm uses critical words, disguised insults, and open blaming of other people to get the upper hand in an argument. Sarcasm can be successfully used and not hurtful when it is good-hearted and meant to be humorous. There is, however, a fine line between good-hearted and mean-spirited sarcasm.

When presented in a mean-spirited manner, sarcasm usually backfires on its user. Studies have shown that while people may agree with the views of a certain speaker, if that person starts spewing sarcasm, listeners will begin to identify with the other viewpoint.

Sarcasm builds resentment in relationships and is considered aggressive behavior because it is not considerate of the needs of others.

Passive Aggression

This behavior is the most subtle and difficult type of anger to handle. The passive-aggressive person is slyly communicating anger while not owning up to it. This category includes behaviors such as the silent treatment, holding grudges, social withdrawal, deliberate ignoring, laziness, procrastination, halfhearted efforts, chronic forgetfulness, or stalling. Rather than dealing with the problem and defusing the anger, passive aggressiveness sabotages constructive communication in a relationship.

Passive aggressiveness backfires on its user as well. While one partner may not be able to prove beyond a shadow of a doubt that the other person is angry, his or her intuition knows that something is going on. But the passive aggressive partner refuses to talk about the real issues, and withdraws and withholds

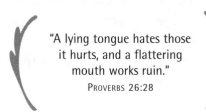

"A lying tongue hates those it hurts, and a flattering mouth works ruin."
PROVERBS 26:28

affection as the relationship gap widens. Eventually real communication ceases entirely.

Humans for the most part are logical beings, but we tend to use logic least in emotional matters. While human intuition is strong and senses passive aggressiveness pretty quickly, people who possess poor intuitive skills will repeatedly be plagued with problematic relationships. Those in whom discernment is skewed to suspect only pure and good motives in other's behavior are known as naïve. Their tendency is to be taken advantage of by others in relationships. This naïveté most often occurs with the lack of age and/or experience in reading people. On the other hand, those who see only questionable and self-serving motives in others are usually extremely jealous and suspicious. Their tendency is to sabotage their own relationships by pushing others away.

Assertiveness

Assertiveness is an attempt to take a stand for personal convictions while continuing to consider the needs of the other people involved. How does someone address anger assertively? By *discussing* your beliefs. That is what dating is about. People who rush quickly into a physical relationship without knowing their partner intimately on an intellectual, spiritual, and emotional level will often end up hurt. We all have expectations associated with intimate relationships that are based in our intellect, spirituality, and emotions. If you don't become aware of those expectations early on, you will likely make huge mistakes both personally and as a couple.

Say no when necessary. This may take some practice, but do it. People who say yes to too many requests can become worn out and start resenting the people they intended to help. Additionally, if they are spread too thin, their help will not live up to the recipients' expectations.

Set firm boundaries. We all have limitations, so why not let them be known? Relationships bloom when both partners can freely express their own boundaries, while respecting the other's boundaries. Again, I recommend the book *Boundaries* by Drs. John Townsend and Henry Cloud; it's one of the classic books of our time about relationships and is a must read for anyone considering marriage.

Openly seek to clarify issues. How many needless conflicts arise from simply misunderstanding each other? Even though you may laugh about the misunderstanding later, the anger it causes at the time can damage the relationship.

Handling issues assertively rather than aggressively will strengthen not only intimate relationships, but *all* your relationships. Your life will change when you realize how much positive influence you can have on your relationships by knowing how to better handle the issues that arise.

Negative Communication/Excessive Criticism

At first glance, verbal abuse does not appear to be nearly as destructive as physical abuse. While males are the primary perpetrators of physical abuse, females tend to fight with their tongues. Verbally berating your mate builds resentment. When verbally attacked, men will often withdraw and detach emotionally from the relationship, often becoming passive-aggressive, which can sometimes be far worse than fighting back verbally.

At times a partner will berate his or her significant other in public, and it can happen in the presence or absence of the partner. This is not only disrespectful, but you are asking for trouble when you begin announcing your partner's flaws to people who might want to inject themselves into your life. Some people respond to conflict in their love lives by actively trying to persuade people to side with them. If this sounds like you (or your partner), then don't be surprised if friends, family, and coworkers don't want to be involved in the business of your love life (though there are some people who *love* to meddle). If anything, they want to remain neutral and on good terms with both parties. Couples who air their dirty laundry in public and try to drag their friends and family into a dispute (making them choose sides) start losing friends quickly.

Recognize also that when you seek "advice" from a friend or family member, you are still in the position of disclosing personal-relationship information to an outside (and almost certainly biased) party. This can not only destroy trust but also open your relationship to the advice and ideas of people who mean well but interject their own agendas into your problem. That might not necessarily be the best for your particular situation. Remember, too, that information you disclose to outside parties may color their opinion of your mate for longer than you would like. Find a trusted counselor or pastor (who understands confidentiality) if you need to seek outside advice. As a couple, make an agreement to never speak in derogatory terms about each other to friends, family, and acquaintances. This protects your relationship and your friendships. Dirty laundry should be kept at home.

The wounds of nasty arguments can heal over time, but the self-esteem of each half of the couple gets a good dousing in the process. If you endure a lot of hurtful arguing during your dating stages, you are increasing your potential for an eventual divorce. Why is divorce mentioned when we're just talking about dating? Because if your dating relationship is filled with drama and hurt, clinicians will tell you that you are in dire jeopardy of having a marriage that will end this way.

Would you like a relationship that others only dream of? Then do this: Make a conscious effort *every day* to build up your partner's self-esteem. Compliment every act of kindness you see in him or her. So many dating and married couples slip into the practice of using their tongues to put the other person down, rather than build the partner up.

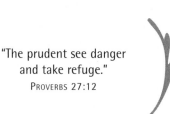

"The prudent see danger and take refuge."
PROVERBS 27:12

Words are extremely powerful tools that can be used to either praise people or punish them. Anger and discontentment often motivate us to use those words. All people in intimate relationships have disagreements and times of discontentment. Putting these factors together shows why guarding your tongue is so essential for a long-term relationship to survive and thrive.

Consider these words of ancient truth:

- "And the tongue is a fire, a world of unrighteousness....
  With it we bless our Lord and Father, and with it we curse
  people who are made in the likeness of God. From the same
  mouth come blessing and cursing. My brothers, these things
  ought not be so." (James 3:6, 9-10, ESV)
- "Let no corrupting talk come out of your mouths, but only
  such as is good for building up, as fits the occasion, that it
  may give grace to those who hear." (Ephesians 4:29, ESV)

Your words wield more power over and meaning to your mate
than anyone else's words. Why is that? Because as couples, we learn
how to push each other's buttons. Few arguments between couples
stay on the original topic but usually degrade into button pushing.
For instance, a girl gets upset with her boyfriend because he's late
picking her up again. She says something to him about it, and he
gets offended. He then says something that he knows will push her
buttons, and off they go.

You can learn to move or remove your buttons, but this process
takes time. And, unfortunately, when you do this, professional button pushers will learn the old methods don't work anymore, so they
find your new ones.

Some couples are addicted to button pushing. These relationships are headed for problems unless the two people figure out why
they are compelled to keep jabbing at each other. Often, jabbing
that starts out mildly escalates into cruel personal stabs. This type
of cancer will truly kill a relationship unless it is brought under
control.

The ideal relationship is one where you know each other's areas
of vulnerability, yet rather than taking advantage of this knowledge,
you both learn to actively help each other strengthen these areas.
The problems of this world attack us every day. How refreshing and
de-stressing it is to have a mate who's on your side. On the flip side,
it can be distressing to have a mate who is adding to your problem
list.

Ryan and Dave were eating dinner with Ryan's family. Dave began receiving text messages on his phone and remarked, "Oh, it's so hard to stay mad at Kari. She is always so sweet when she says she's sorry."

Ryan couldn't help pointing out the problem. "You better be careful. Just because she says she's sorry doesn't mean she is!"

Ryan was right in this case. Kari and Dave had many daily arguments, generally leaving Dave with the blame for all the problems in the free world. He could do nothing right. Had Dave and Kari engaged in minimal disagreements over time, Ryan would not have made his comment.

Ryan then made a second comment to Dave. "Just because she says she's sorry doesn't mean you need to keep her around."

Again, Ryan was right in this case. Ryan realized that Kari loved conflict and never took responsibility for anything. In the end Dave broke off his relationship with Kari.

Remember, as in the case of Kari and Dave, a sweet apology after continuing conflict is abusive. A person does not need to hit or slap to be abusive. A person who continually inflicts verbal chaos and conflict into a relationship is abusing his or her partner. A sweet apology after constant chaos and blaming is no different from the apology of a man who brings his wife flowers after he hits her. The core issue is the same, and you will be wise to recognize it before you get into trouble for good.

Selfishness

As humans, we are all born selfish, and it shows up early in life. For example, a friend gave a birthday party for her five-year-old son, and when it was time to play a game, all the kids started asking, "Can I go first?" When the cake and ice cream arrived, there was again a mass pleading of "me first" from the party participants.

Kids are selfish, yet most of the time we don't hold it against them because we expect kids to act this way. Adults, however, are supposed to learn somewhere between childhood and adulthood (perhaps during adolescence) the value of selflessness. The problem is that no matter how many times we learn this lesson, our human tendency toward selfishness will be a constant source of struggle in our relationships. But by acknowledging this battle and committing to work together to change, you and your partner can see victory in your moment-by-moment decisions to be selfless.

Besides being born selfish, many children are subject to well-meaning parents who actually reinforce selfish behavior in their children. One sure way to produce a self-centered adult is to give him everything he wants as a kid, without his ever having to earn anything. Rather than stimulating an "attitude of gratitude," it creates a sense of entitlement. Selfishness is further reinforced when children and adolescents are neglected, causing them to ultimately want to take whatever they can to meet their every need, real or imagined. The problem is they never learned balance in this area, so they take and take, yet never feel satisfied.

Every person possesses some degree of selfishness. It becomes a problem in relationships when the giving and taking is lopsided. Good relationships bring out the giving nature of both partners. This often spills over into better relationships with other people as well.

CRAM FOR THE EXAM

A well-known relationship "expert" once likened marriage to "the toughest and longest test in life." That may well be true. And if you're taking a test in school, what greatly improves your odds for success? Studying for the exam. So, too, studying for the test of marriage is a wise decision. But how does one study for something like a marriage relationship?

The key to effective studying is anticipating what questions the professor will ask and then learning the answers to those questions. Getting a high grade in the test of marriage, then, might consist of knowing what relationship questions to ask and then answering them.

The number one question is, "Can I commit to loving and caring for this person the rest of my life?" Here are six more questions to ponder before making that step:

1. Can I live with this person the way he or she is now? (There's no guarantee that your partner will ever be any better than now.)
2. Do I have the freedom with this person to do and say what is truly on my heart?
3. Is my partner kind and affirming? Do I feel safe with him or her?
4. Is our communication:
   a. meaningful?
   b. deep when necessary?
   c. reassuring?
5. Can I trust this person to keep our marriage faithful?
6. Are we both willing to put each other first in our relationship?

If you can answer these with a confident "yes," then you are well on your way to a great marriage relationship.

Reality Check

Take time with the questions at the end of this chapter and carefully consider your responses. If any major issues come up with a person you are now dating, think about having an honest discussion about those issues.

Write It Down

What are your hot buttons that easily get pushed?

What buttons do you find yourself pushing most in others?

What steps will you take to remove your buttons?

What steps will you take to stop being a button pusher?

If you continually connect with button pushers, list why you attract those people to your life.

(7)

Recognizing the Red Flags

Singles say…

> …they ignored the red flags in a relationship by dismissing them as having potential to be overcome.

> …poor morals of the friends and/or families of dating partners were found to be predictors of poor morality and character defects of the dating partner.

> …they have stayed in a comfort zone far too long to the detriment of at least one significant relationship.

Dan is a man who was abused by his mother. It is no surprise that he eventually married, twice, women who were emotionally and verbally abusive to him. After years of therapy, Dan became a master at understanding the kinds of friends, coworkers, and romantic partners he should have in his life. Red flags were easy for Dan to spot in his relationships, and the years of therapy caused him to be a stellar person himself.

Finally Dan met an amazing woman, full of every quality he admired. He got to know her strengths and weaknesses, and they began to pursue the idea of marriage. The couple agreed on absolutely everything imaginable—from family interactions to money decisions, living arrangements to grocery shopping. Dan and Melonie agreed that should they ever have a major disagreement or need special assistance, they would immediately seek counseling. They went through premarital counseling and felt good about their future partnership.

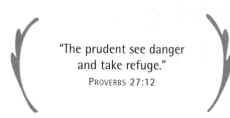

"The prudent see danger and take refuge."
PROVERBS 27:12

The day before the wedding Melonie's family arrived. As the couple toasted each other at the rehearsal dinner, they said many heartfelt things. During Melonie's toast, she told family and friends this was the beginning of a journey to include wedded bliss, a houseful of children, and growing old together. Imagine Dan's shock, since the couple had agreed they would never have children.

Dan was bothered by Melonie's blatant lie to her family but resolved to discuss the issue after the wedding. The wedding and honeymoon came and went, and finally Dan brought up the topic. Melonie told Dan she'd only agreed to not have children to appease him, thinking she could change his mind after the wedding.

While Dan had seen the huge red flag waving during their rehearsal-dinner toast, he was so shocked and taken aback—especially due to the timing—that he did not think of calling the wedding off. Dan realized that if Melonie had made her comment a week or two before the wedding, he would have dealt with it then or called off the wedding if the question wasn't resolved. His failure to react to this red flag resulted in years of heartache that ended in yet another divorce.

It's much better to deal with red flags in a relationship early—instead of after the wedding. A red flag is a warning, much like a red light. When confronted with a red flag, you need to stop and look around to assess the safety of moving forward in the relationship. Like disease and wildfire, a red flag is ignored at your peril.

In this chapter we'll consider some common red flags that crop up early in relationships and can serve as wake-up calls to dangers ahead.

RED FLAG #1: EXPECTING TO CHANGE A WOLF INTO A SHEEP

Do you have the power to change another person? No; the only person you can change is yourself. Coming to grips with this reality can change your whole life dramatically (for the better). Do we have the power to show another person how to change and help him change? You bet! But there is one huge condition: That person must want to change, and demonstrate it *consistently*.

Remember this important fact: If someone has to change a great deal in order to continue in a relationship with you, you probably abandoned most of your "wish list" when you began dating that person. Review your list and ask yourself if you are trying to make a square peg fit through a round hole. If this is not the first relationship where someone had to make dramatic changes to satisfy your prerequisites, you need to ask yourself why you keep selecting the wrong type of person, then forcing him or her to change to fit your wish list.

"I thought she would change" is a common statement heard by relationship counselors. Be careful committing to someone on the assumption that he or she will change. Wait first for the change to occur, then wait some more. Does the change last? If someone changes just to please you, that change probably won't last. For true lasting change, that person must have the will and desire to change to become a better person, with or without you.

Keep in mind that there are people walking around in this world who look and act a lot like you but who are mentally unbalanced. We in the mental-health profession see these people put on great fronts, but within a short time the red flags start appearing. Do not discern the heart of another person based on *your* reality. Realize that with the increased dysfunction in our society, there are people out there whose realities are warped. Serious disorders are multiplying, and some of the symptoms are quite subtle: manipulation, lying, and the ability to suck you in because you are a nice person.

> "Great beginnings are not as important as the way one finishes."
> DR. JAMES DOBSON

Do not dismiss the red flags, and do not attempt to "fix" the people you decide to date. Many of these people can change only with the help of a team of qualified professionals.

Sticking to your goal, following your own path in life, and requiring your dating relationships to fit into that path will help you avoid these dysfunctional people. If you do date someone who tries to suck you into her chaos, she'll eventually go away if you take things slowly, stick to your goals, and stay on your path. This is a tried-and-true test for weeding out unhealthy people before you get in too deep.

The costs of ignoring a major red flag were paid by a pastor we'll call Roger. He hoped to change his wife, but that hope was not fulfilled.

Clarise and Roger had a wonderful dating and engagement relationship. A few weeks before the wedding Roger asked Clarise to keep her bachelorette party clean.

Clarise had wanted to go to a male strip club with her friends (only because it was their suggestion), but she promised Roger she would change plans and do something less sexual in nature. Roger was in seminary and was pleased that Clarise respected his future career, and he was relieved to hear that she had only agreed to the club idea because her friends wanted her to go. The wedding day arrived, and Roger learned from the husband of a bridesmaid that Clarise had, in fact, gone to a strip club where she got drunk and acted like a "girl gone wild."

The sexual nature of the event did not, in and of itself, bother Roger. He trusted Clarise to be faithful to him. What really bothered Roger was that Clarise had lied to him. For Roger, finding out the lie ruined his wedding day. It also led to a honeymoon of turmoil. Clarise refused to understand that caving in to the wishes of her friends put them ahead of Roger.

During the next five years of their marriage, the pattern of Clarise's putting her family, friends, job, and just about anything else before Roger continued. She would consistently agree over issues with Roger but at the last minute give in to the whims of other people. The relationship ended, and Roger ended up a divorced pastor.

Roger states that he knew on the day of the wedding he should have called it off. He trusted, however, that with counseling they could resolve anything. Clarise's behavior never changed, and although Roger never wanted to divorce Clarise, she proved to be completely untrustworthy, and he could not trust her in any area, even with the counselor's help. Roger made the call to end the relationship, though it went against everything he believed. He said he would have attempted to stay longer had he not been a pastor, but in the church he could not stay true to his ministry and attempt to save a marriage when his wife refused to work with both him and the counselor.

RED FLAG #2: NEEDINESS

All humans have needs. No one is self-sufficient. In fact, there is great benefit in needing others and meeting others' needs. One thing people need is affection. There is nothing wrong with this natural need unless it becomes controlling. Looking too intently to others for affirmation can actually be counterproductive and push those same people away. While other people can have a profound effect on our moods and contentment, no human has the power to make us feel good all the time.

Needy people demand that others make them happy. When this doesn't happen, they become more demanding and then critical. Ironically, neediness ends up producing the opposite effect of what is desired. Forcing others to focus on your needs *first* makes them not want to. When they do, it is usually begrudgingly. When you focus on pleasing another person first, that person will usually want to please you in turn. What if that's not the case? Then you may consider having second thoughts about the future of an intimate relationship with this person.

> "I don't think much of a man who is not wiser today than he was yesterday."
> ABRAHAM LINCOLN

Needy people strive for superiority in every relationship—the extreme form of it being domination. If they get the slightest hint that they are being placed in an inferior position, anger and protest ensue. They will make statements like, "I hate being treated like a nobody," or, "All you ever do is talk down to me," or the clincher, "I feel so unloved." These statements are emotional blackmail, and these people always play the one-up position. While they behave like meek wallflowers on the outside, their manipulative motives are at work on the inside. Beware! Another tactic needy people commonly employ is making negative comments publicly about others. There are few things more destructive to a relationship than one partner publicly putting down the other one. Remember, "in public" also includes posting intimate details of your relationship or perceived behavior on Myspace or Facebook Web sites.

Many relationships thrive on a paradox. This paradox is that by focusing on meeting the needs of and affirming the other, each one discovers his or her own needs are met and affirmation is received. If you are always trying to serve your mate, and you are still in the one-down position, then the two of you are coming from dramatically different perspectives. Evaluate the risks of moving forward with this relationship.

RED FLAG #3: FEELINGS ADDICTION OR RELATIONSHIP ADDICTION

Many people do not realize that feelings are controllable. "That's just how I feel" or "That is just how I was made" are common statements people use to justify their out-of-control emotions. Feelings can be controlled and, with practice, most people find their lives enhanced greatly when they are able to do it well. People who allow their feelings to control them are actually not showing their true personalities. Feelings that overrun a person cover up true personality.

Have you ever known someone who is dramatic and feelings oriented? The real person can rarely be seen under all those feelings. Picture your dating partner totally covered in a blanket. Introduce this date to people, and all they are left saying is, "Nice blanket!" Of course this is a silly exaggeration, but it is exactly what you are doing when you date a feelings addict.

Feelings addicts are almost always unhappy and hurting within most of their relationships—dating, family, and friends. The highs are high, but the lows are debilitating, and not just to the feelings addicts but also to anyone with whom they are involved. If you are a feelings addict, you are seeing the world through your feelings, which distorts the reality of most situations you are in. It's as bad as wearing glasses that distort your vision. You will be unable to select great friends and dates if you cannot clearly see the people you are selecting. Always feeling victimized is common in people who allow their feelings to rule their lives.

If you are dating a feelings addict, you have no idea who that person really is. Do not believe that you can change the person either. There is a reason he or she is this way, and it likely goes far back into childhood. A feelings addict might temporarily change for the better to appease you, but it will require some heavy acting that cannot be sustained. Only with intense therapy can this person truly change for the better. If you want to help, refer him to a counselor or clergy person, then back off the relationship so he can get help. He will not be able to focus on helping himself if he's also attempting to maintain a dating relationship.

> "Never mistake knowledge for wisdom. One helps you make a living; the other helps you make a life."
> SANDRA CAREY

If he never likes any of his counselors, recognize that this is another symptom of feelings addicts. Everyone, including physicians, clergy, and therapists, will "hurt their feelings." Until they learn to hear and accept the truth, they will never heal. Understand this as you form relationships in the future.

Besides feelings addiction, you need to be aware that relationship addiction, yours or your partner's, is extremely unhealthy. If you feel you must have another person in your life to be happy, you are a candidate for relationship addiction. In fact, when you learn how to be truly happy alone, you'll begin to be the most successful in every relationship.

RED FLAG #4: UNREALISTIC EXPECTATIONS

We all have expectations—intellectual, spiritual, emotional—associated with our intimate relationships. If you don't become aware of those expectations early on, you will likely make huge mistakes both personally and as a couple. Many expectations are valid and healthy. But beware of the following unrealistic expectations:

Sex Will Improve the Relationship

What do two people in a dysfunctional, nonsexual relationship get when they start having sex? A dysfunctional relationship that's now sexual. Love is not sex, and sex is not love. Sex will not create intimacy in a relationship. Rather, sex should be the culmination, or celebration, of intimacy in a committed relationship—marriage.

Sexual activity before commitment leads to distrust of the other person. It can also bring on feelings of guilt, shame, and depression. Sex only builds up the relationship when there is total commitment and intimacy in the context of marriage. If this is missing, sexual activity will ultimately begin tearing down the relationship.

Anecdotal reports show a poor success rate among dating couples who try to stop sexual activity once they've started it.

Children Will Improve the Relationship

Children are a wonderful blessing, but they are also hard work and put strain on a relationship. An already-strained relationship can break under the added pressure of a child. Not only does a child negatively affect a strained relationship, but a strained relationship negatively affects that child, often for life. Obviously parents survive and even enjoy having children—most couples have more than one. But if you think having a baby or taking on stepchildren will improve a poor relationship, ask some of your own family members what they think. You might be surprised at their willingness to share their experiences in order to save you pain in life. You need to know this information before deciding to marry someone.

Differences in Expectations Don't Matter

We all have expectations about how our relationships should look. An important question is, "How closely do your expectations match the other person's?" A skilled marketing person claims the key to a happy customer is not just a good product, but also managing the customer's expectations about that product on the front end. If I buy a lawnmower expecting it to trim my shrubs, my expectation for the product is different from the manufacturer's. I will be disappointed in the product and may get mangled if I use it to trim the shrubs.

It is easy to see the problem of differing expectations with products, but we must do the same thing in relationships. Just because something seems obvious to you does not mean it makes sense for a person with whom you enter into a relationship.

What do you expect in a husband or wife? Your potential mate should closely fit the wish list you were encouraged to make several chapters ago. Have you asked your date if you fit his or her wish list? (Make sure you're in the right disclosure stage of the relationship before you ask this question, or you might send your dating partner running for his or her life.)

A man may say he wants his potential spouse to be happy and pursue a career or run her own business. He really might mean it in theory. What if, however, he has some internal belief that a good husband will earn enough pay to keep his wife at home and take care of all of her needs? You guessed it. When they finally marry, there will be conflict over her working, because it makes him feel like less of a man. This may sound like a conventional example, but marriage counselors will tell you this situation happens more often than you would expect in this day of equality for women.

Family-of-Origin Expectations Don't Matter

How does a female who grew up wealthy with an unlimited budget fare when dating a man who grew up poor and who realizes the value of a dollar? Issues like these impact relationships much more than most couples realize before they are married. The top three areas of marital strife are (1) money, (2) sex, and (3) raising children. It's important for couples to consider their different expectations when deciding whether to marry.

Many couples go into marriage barely considering the top few conflicts and tend to take a wait-and-see approach. Professional athletic teams practice and strategize by watching their opponents' game films prior to hitting the field on game day. Can you imagine how much more successful you would be in all your relationships if you prepared this way? A wait-and-see mentality

> "I am sending you out like sheep among wolves. Therefore be as shrewd as snakes and as innocent as doves."
> Matthew 10:16

would be disaster for the athlete, and it's even worse for you in your closest interpersonal relationship.

What does your family expect from a potential mate for you, and what does his or her family expect from you? These are questions that need to be asked so that if disagreements arise, they can be addressed before you make the commitment to marry.

Deciding on how holidays will be spent is an expectation that needs to be addressed before marriage. This issue might seem like a no-brainer to some couples, but to many it can be a source of stress.

Did you know that in-laws are on the list of the top five causes of marital strife?

A good premarital counselor can help you create a plan agreeable to each of you regarding your leisure time, money, and family issues. There are emotional ties and expectations surrounding holidays, birthdays, and other special days, so couples must present a united front before those special days turn into nightmares.

In order to have harmony in your relationship as a couple, seek to understand the personality of each person's family. Does your partner come from a family that is vastly different from yours? If so, what seems like a new, interesting, and unique situation can ultimately wreck your upcoming marriage. Use the dating experience to begin looking closely at your significant other's family. Ask yourself the following: Could I move into this home and totally embrace living the way they live? (Let's hope that never has to happen.) If you look at your dating partner's family in this manner, you can begin discussing what a successful household looks like should you make the trip down the aisle. Even if you have not progressed to the disclosure stage where you and your dating partner should have this discussion, you'll want to look closely at this area.

> "Above all else, guard your heart, for it is the wellspring of life."
> PROVERBS 4:23

One thing many new couples never consider is what to do when parents become too frail to care for themselves. You may have differing ideas on this subject, with neither one being necessarily wrong. Say a rift occurs after marriage when a decision must be made about helping older parents in need. This scenario could be avoided if you discuss these things before you take that stroll down the aisle. There are four phases in life: You start out as your parents' child, then you become your child's parent. Next you become your parents' parent, then you progress to the last stage of being your children's child. Yikes! Potential mates should spend ample time in discussing all four phases.

No two families do things exactly alike. You and your future spouse are no exception. If you choose to marry, you will form a distinct family separate from your families of origin. Are you both willing to recognize that and accept the responsibility?

Momma's boys and Daddy's girls have a difficult time in marriage relationships. Their enmeshed connection to their parents basically brings a third person into the marriage, and three is definitely a crowded marriage. If you are dating someone who has not sufficiently separated from his or her parents, be careful before you consider marrying that person. Trying to force him or her to pick you over family rarely works but instead makes the family resent you even more. Is your partner able to realize on his or her own that it's time to move on and start a family, a family that will be different from the parents' family?

Kristy dated Stan for months, and she did her homework. Having read many self-help books and having analyzed her past relationships, she felt Stan might be the perfect guy. They had similar family backgrounds, and just about everything on her "list" was represented in Stan. As they became more serious, she admired Stan's commitment to his parents and his love for his much-younger siblings. Kristy felt great love and commitment for her own parents and siblings, and she saw their family values as complementary.

Kristy became a bit concerned when Stan's undying affection for his stepfather appeared to be more than what she felt it should be, but she dismissed her concern as paranoia. Stan made comments about how he would love to help his family pay for his younger siblings' college expenses. He felt this would be possible since he would have graduated from law school and be working in a law practice by the time the siblings reached college age. Kristy thought this was great, because at times she fantasized about ways in which she could be a blessing to her own family.

A holiday with Stan's family gave Kristy the missing piece of the puzzle that raised the red flag regarding Stan and his clan. Kristy learned that Stan's family was paying for his college and law school, with the expectation that he would, in turn, pay for his younger siblings' educations. Kristy clarified this with Stan, and he admitted that was the agreement. Kristy immediately explained that they could no longer see each other.

Though Kristy had no intention of marrying anyone soon, she explained to Stan that by guaranteeing to pay both kids' tuition, he would not be able to start a life with a woman for years down the road. Additionally, Kristy felt the bigger issue was the disrespect shown by Stan's parents regarding his future. Stan did not see it that way, and Kristy counted it as a good learning experience about an overly connected family system.

What happens when couples from totally different cultures marry? These marriages can and do work at times, and they are often rewarding for both families, but it's critical to plan and communicate before the marriage happens. Cultural diversity adds interest and dimension to a family, but it can also bring about its share of conflicts based on unspoken expectations. Look into cultural issues, such as gender roles and religious and spiritual differences, before you progress into a deeper stage of a relationship with someone from a different culture than yours.

If you are dating someone and dealing with a challenging family member, a comprehensive handbook for you is *Who's Pushing Your Buttons?* by Dr. John Townsend. This book explains why difficult people exhibit negative behaviors, and it also prepares the reader for effectively dealing with the person(s) and the problem(s).

Address these problems before you walk the aisle. Later you'll be glad you did.

RED FLAG #5: JEALOUSY

Sandi spent a lot of time building up Perry with compliments and buying him gifts. She constantly asked him if he would like company on his errands or when he was studying. Perry felt good having someone appreciate his gifts and talents, and Sandi seemed sweet to offer to spend time with him during boring tasks. Because Sandi constantly flattered his talents, Perry quickly fell into thinking he was her knight in shining armor.

Soon the two were spending nearly all their waking hours together. When Perry was with family or friends, Sandi called and sent text messages several times an hour. Usually she would tell him the messages were to help plan what they would do later.

Over the next two years, this behavior grew into full-blown jealousy to the point that when Perry was at school or with family or friends, she accused him of "cheating" on her. She sabotaged Perry's education whenever she could by feigning problems that only he could fix. Finally, because Perry took a day to mow a sick neighbor's yard and she was so jealous he wasn't with her, she decided to "pay him back" and cheated on him.

Not surprisingly, for months after the breakup, Sandi begged Perry to come back, still blaming him for not meeting her overly dependent needs.

Fortunately, the issue in the story above was resolved before this couple decided to marry. All too often individuals don't see the subtle signs of jealousy while they are creeping up. Jealous people hide their jealousy because they know how ugly it is.

Jealousy comes from only one thing: insecurity. A secure person has his or her own life and doesn't need anyone else for completion. If you are being asked to be someone's "everything," you're in a dangerous spot. All of us will hurt someone at sometime, even if we don't mean to. But because a jealous person sees the world through "victim" eyes, almost everything you do outside of that person will be considered hurtful to him or her. Make no mistake—a jealous person will not just be jealous of other people. They'll be jealous of anything that takes time away from them. They want the reassurance of being physically or emotionally connected with their dating partners all day, every day. No person can be the source of completing someone and meeting all their needs this way.

> "Like a gold ring in a pig's snout is a beautiful woman who shows no discretion."
> PROVERBS 11:22

Sandi's flattery in the beginning was her way of demonstrating to Perry that she needed reassurance. Understand that the way a person treats you is generally a huge indication of how he or she wants to be treated in return. Constant flattery is flattering, but a person who does this believes *you need it*. Why? Because *he or she needs it* and cannot see the world from anyone else's perspective.

Flattery serves one other purpose for the jealous person. It serves to make you feel good about yourself, thereby solidifying the jealous person's hold on you. Everyone has a need to feel admired, and the jealous person knows how to tap into that need.

In the end, Sandi punished Perry by cheating on him—the ultimate betrayal. She even said Perry caused her infidelity by not being with her, and she fully expected him to understand her reasoning.

Are jealous people sinister? It would seem that way, but in reality they are so insecure that their entire view of the world is colored by green-colored glasses. Relationships built on the foundation of jealousy will always fail unless the jealous person receives professional help. Even so, the prognosis is not good for the jealous person, and if success does come, it will only come over time.

Remember, dating continues until the moment you say, "I do." Regardless of the timing, address red-flag issues as if you had one more year before the big day. Unfortunately, the true character of a person can come out at the worst possible time. A person who is attempting to meet his or her own needs may attempt to pull the wool over your eyes until the very last moment. Most people don't do this because they are bad or evil; they are just insecure or self-centered.

As soon as you do identify a red flag in your dating relationship, take action, no matter how difficult or how late in the game it might be.

Reality Check/Write It Down

Put a check mark next to the red-flag warning signs you have ignored in the past.

_____ Partner needs serious changing.

_____ Partner is overly needy.

_____ Partner is addicted to feelings or relationships.

_____ Unrealistic expectations are present.

_____ Sex will improve the relationship.

_____ Children will improve the relationship.

_____ Differences in expectations don't matter.

_____ Differences in family-of-origin expectations don't matter.

_____ Partner is a jealous person.

For each of the previous categories, go back and mark down how many times you have done these things in past dating relationships.

Analyze whether you also ignore some of these red flags with friends and coworkers. If your answer is no, ask your best friend or a trusted relative if they see you exhibiting the same behaviors in all your relationships.

(8)

Getting to "I Do"

Singles say…

> …they talk themselves out of their plans two to three times before they go into more permanent action.
>
> …their problematic relationships were always spotted by outside parties before the singles "got it" on their own.
>
> …they have compromised their values in relationships to get someone they thought they wanted.

Congratulations—you're still studying this book, having learned about relationship cancers, false assumptions, red flags, and other dating pitfalls. We've looked at stages encountered during early dating and engagement. This chapter will help you learn more about making the final commitment and dealing with a few more issues that can crop up at this point in a relationship.

MAKING THE DECISION

People make marriage decisions for many different reasons or motivations. Sadly, some people later regret their ill-conceived decision-making process, or they realize they didn't follow what their consciences were telling them to do. Other people simply marry when they are too young to understand the depth of the promise and commitment they are making.

Even our physical wiring can interfere with good decision-making. While human physical ability peaks between 16 and 18 years of age, learning ability peaks around 18 to 22 years of age. During this phase the brain can add billions of new synapses and the ability to remember and recall is improved. Wisdom ability is the third type of growth and the slowest to occur. It concerns the part of the brain that allows us to plan, make decisions, and reason properly. It doesn't usually peak until at least age 25. A person whose wisdom ability has not fully matured is prone to make impulsive decisions and errors in judgment. This helps explain why a perfectly intelligent 20-year-old can still make poor decisions.

Let's consider some ill-advised ways people make the marriage decision.

Asking God to Baptize Your Decision

"Love is blind" is an old cliché expressing the romanticized idea that we overlook the bad for the good within the object of our love. "Dear Lord, I'm asking Claire to marry me tonight. Please make her the right one." Making a decision and then asking God to approve it is backward, yet that's how many people proceed. It is far better to begin by seeking God's will for your life.

What does it mean to seek God's will for your marriage partner and your life? In Romans 12:2, we find this direction: "Do not conform any longer to the pattern of this world, but be transformed by the renewing of your mind. Then you will be able to test and approve what God's will is—his good, pleasing and perfect will."

By ignoring the world's patterns for relationships (review chapter 1 on false assumptions and chapter 2 on the three forms of love), you will have cleared the ground for making a wise choice of a mate. By transforming yourself by the renewing of your mind (review chapter 3 on knowing yourself), you will be more likely to be a good candidate for marriage. Lastly, you can test God's will by answering all the common-sense questions offered in this book. You may still make a mistake, but you'll be far ahead of the crowd in making a successful marriage choice.

Asking God to Make Your Decision for You

People sometimes make statements about their dating relationships such as, "Well if it's meant to be, then it will be. If it's not, then it's not. There's nothing I can do about it." These are generally the same people who don't wear seat belts or motorcycle helmets because, they say, "If it's my time to die, then I will die anyway." The same is true of couples in relationship trouble. Those with the attitude that "God will break us up or keep us together" don't generally end up in fabulous relationships.

We humans have free will, which includes the ability to reason, choose, and make our own decisions. The people who sit around waiting for deci-

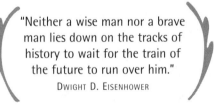

"Neither a wise man nor a brave man lies down on the tracks of history to wait for the train of the future to run over him."
DWIGHT D. EISENHOWER

sions to be made for them will often be disappointed. Why would someone enjoy *not* making his or her own decisions? Perhaps the person is afraid to take responsibility for a decision in case it turns out to be a bad one.

Let's consider faulty assumptions regarding taking responsibility for one's life. If you believe that God is God, you also likely believe that He can do anything He pleases. If you believe in Him, even in small part, then you probably believe that He can and does intervene in people's lives at times. Many have seen evidence of this when they face situations over which they truly have no power. But that doesn't mean we abdicate our responsibility to make logical, wise decisions using our own God-given mental and emotional abilities.

"Spiritualization" and "manipulation" are two psychological terms that describe how people try to push the responsibility for their decisions off on God. "Spiritualization" is basically the baptized form of "rationalization." For instance, Jennifer reasons that God must want her to stay in a relationship with Rob because Rob has not broken up with her. Now, her unhappiness in the relationship has a reason: God must want it. It also takes away her responsibility to improve the relationship or get out of it. At least that is what she tells herself.

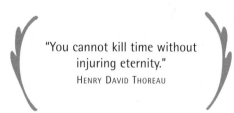

"You cannot kill time without injuring eternity."
HENRY DAVID THOREAU

Sarah used manipulation tactics with God in her decisions. She would contemplate a choice, then say, "Okay, God, You decide this for me." Next she looked at the automobiles around her. If she saw a white car, then God's answer was yes, but if she saw a black one first, that meant His answer was no. Sometimes she would do this two or three times to make sure the answer was right. Testing God just does not work. We cannot force an omnipotent being to answer us by sending messages through contrived scenarios.

Those who take responsibility for their own decisions and use the tools they've been given will make the best choices—not only when selecting a dating partner or spouse, but in all of life's decisions.

Letting Someone Else Make Your Decisions

Allowing someone else to make your decisions (especially in a bad relationship) causes a phenomenon called "hostile dependency." One partner chooses to be dependent on the other but is resentful or angry about that dependency.

Getting counsel from friends and family who know and love you concerning your life decisions is wise. Just remember, it is easy for another person to tell you what to do or not do, but you are the one who has to live with those decisions once the wedding and honeymoon are over. If things go sour, those people who told you to go for it will rarely take the blame. In fact, they might even say things like, "I knew all along you never should have married her." Their memories become very short.

Make your own decisions because you are the one who will be affected the most by them. A note of caution: If just about everyone you know is telling you there is a serious problem with your choice of a dating partner, listen. After examining the evidence, see a counselor so you are certain you are seeing all sides of the picture, then make a decision equipped with good insight. This could save you from making a terrible mistake.

Deciding Under Pressure

Brittany claimed she had a plan all worked out that would end her relationship with John gently. It was John's senior year of college, and he would be graduating in a few months. He planned to move to New Jersey and pursue a master's degree. Brittany had one more year of college, and she hoped the relationship would fade away during the year John was gone.

"I wouldn't count on it," were her father's words.

Brittany's passivity did soon put her in a pickle. John announced a few weeks before graduation that he had decided not to move to New Jersey but instead would spend the year working, allowing him to get some real life experience while waiting for Brittany to graduate. John showed up unannounced at Brittany's family reunion, had the DJ call Brittany up front, got down on his knee, and proposed to her in front of dozens of family members. All Brittany could do at that moment was gasp a yes then almost faint when her family members began shouting and clapping. Her parents clapped but, knowing the real situation, they were close to passing out as well.

Once engaged, Brittany told her family that she had changed her mind and did want to marry John. The family supported her and provided a beautiful wedding but not without counseling her that she was making a huge mistake. Brittany told them she just couldn't hurt John's feelings. Soon after the wedding Brittany became pregnant and later confided to her mother that she now knew she had made a mistake.

John insisted on moving to New Jersey to pursue his master's degree. Brittany found herself hundreds of miles away from her family for the first time in her life and quite lonesome. Brittany's mother cried every time she got off the phone with Brittany, because her daughter sounded so lonely. Brittany's mother also blamed herself, saying, "Why didn't I do more to try and stop this marriage?"

Continuing to exclusively date someone you don't intend to marry is more hurtful to both of you than ending the relationship. It's a form of deception. Not only that, it's a time waster and an opportunity for an even bigger mistake, as happened to Brittany and John. It can also lead you off of your life's best path. Yes, people do grow on other people after a while, but if you're to the point of talking about marriage and the other person has not yet grown on you, consider that a huge red flag. Also consider the fact that as you continue to date the wrong person, you are missing opportunities to find that person who truly "fits your wish list."

Deciding by Emotions or Reason?

All too often, relationships are ruled by emotions, and reason takes second place where romance is concerned. You discover perfect examples of this on the many TV reality shows as they portray a wide range of dramatic feelings linked to the process of "falling in love." These programs reveal people who display happiness, excitement, rejection, despair, anger, and even self-deception. The variety and strength of these emotions is astounding.

Emotions have one thing in common: they are always in a constant state of change. Emotionally healthy people are aware of their feelings and listen to them quite often, but don't live by them. What if you lived by your feelings when it came to education and only went to class or studied when you felt like it? What if you lived by your feelings about your job and only went to work when you wanted to? What if you ate every time you saw something appetizing? You would be failing, fired, and fat.

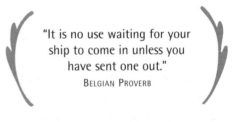

"It is no use waiting for your ship to come in unless you have sent one out."
BELGIAN PROVERB

Our brain chemistry can distort our emotions. Slight hormone changes can trigger powerful emotions. Fatigue, the weather, and arguments can all affect our emotions. Emotions can also be outright deceiving and are difficult to control, but some people manage to succeed in this area much better than others. How do they do it?

They know that emotions often change when behavior changes. If you remember only one sentence from this book, make it this next one, for it will change your life: "You can act your way into a better way of feeling, better than you can feel your way into a better way of acting."

Take exercising, for example. If you sat around and waited until you felt like running five miles, you might never go. But if you decide that you will start running at 5:30 P.M., regardless of how you feel, you will be glad when you finish. Your feelings will follow your actions. People whose actions follow their feelings will be in for a roller-coaster ride in life and will endure disappointment about never reaching their full potential. Every time you push yourself to step out and do something uncomfortable, you are sending a message to yourself that flows into every aspect of your life.

Your personality can also play a part in how much you rely on reason or emotions to make your marriage decisions. Two personality factors that radically affect behavior are impulsivity and compulsivity.

> "Most of the shadows of this life are caused by standing in one's own sunshine."
> RALPH WALDO EMERSON

Impulsive people act on their emotions, which often gets them into trouble. They are people who blurt out what they think before thinking about the impact of their words. They are known to experience more problems with, among other areas, maintaining relationships. They will also charge into fearful situations (such as marriage) where others will move slowly. Impulsivity is found on a continuum, and no one is 100 percent impulsive. People on the more impulsive end of the line tend to be more emotional.

People who fall on the compulsive end of the continuum are not as daring, are more calculating, and prefer to adhere to structure. Compulsive people follow reason and logic more than emotions. If the speed limit is 25 mph, they will daringly go 26—but no faster! While compulsive personalities have numerous positive traits, they can also be stubborn and hard to deal with. Many times there is only one way to do it right—*their* way. They also tend to be more argumentative, be more negative, and stay angry longer if their feelings are hurt. Some can hold a grudge forever after being wronged.

We all fall somewhere on the impulsive/compulsive continuum. The healthiest personalities have both qualities. Personalities on either extreme are unhealthy and difficult to deal with in long-term intimate relationships. Someone who's too impulsive, for example, may be a barrel of fun to hang out with but is always broke. Marrying this person would mean placing yourself in a position to struggle in many areas of your life. Usually this person is just as broke on a salary of one million dollars as he is on twenty-five thousand (he just has more toys at one million). A mate on the compulsive extreme could pinch every penny so hard that it would be just the same as living broke with the impulsive spouse.

Emotionally healthy people acknowledge their own feelings and traits, both positive and negative, and equally acknowledge the feelings and traits of their partner. This includes evaluation of just how impulsive or compulsive both you and your dating partner tend to be. Discern what brings out positive and negative emotions, as well as each other's tendencies toward impulsivity and compulsivity. This will be important in understanding how those issues will enhance or erode the relationship over time.

Emotions are often positive, and we should pay attention to them. Don't, however, make lifelong decisions based on a surge of emotion that could be the result of a hormone release, anger, excitement, or exhaustion.

Avoiding Overdependence

Expect a sunny day, but don't forget an umbrella or you may wind up soaked. This good advice also holds true for relationships. Rather than seeing this as a pessimistic mind-set, consider this advice in the same way as you would view insurance. Does getting home insurance mean you plan for your house to burn down? No, but you will be left sleeping on the street if it does and you aren't insured.

How does this concept apply in relationships? You can be susceptible to a downpour with no protection if you put yourself in the position of becoming overly dependent on the other person in your relationship. The three most common types of overdependence we see in relationships are physical, financial, and emotional. In Jill's case, her dependence was emotional, though her boyfriend's dependence was physical.

> Jerrod asked Jill to marry him after knowing her for less than one month. When Jerrod flunked out of college (mainly from skipping class to feed his computer-game addiction), his parents cut him off financially. Rather than discontinuing his daily computer antics and securing employment, he simply asked Jill if he could move in with her for a while. Jill said no because she didn't feel right living with a guy outside of marriage.
>
> The next day Jerrod purchased a very small ring and announced he was moving in by the weekend. Jill compromised her values because she felt if she said no to the proposal, Jerrod might dump her. She also felt guilty because he was about to be homeless.
>
> Jerrod came to his senses and recognized that he and Jill were not made for each other. He moved out, but not without a great deal of hurt. Jill realized that if she had stuck to her guns, Jerrod may have cleaned up his act much sooner and become a responsible adult, and they might possibly have ended up together in a healthy marriage.

Just as it's important not to become dependent on the other person, don't allow someone else to become dependent on you. Remember, if the relationship ends because you won't compromise your principles, it wasn't worth keeping.

Commingling finances before marriage is another area of over-dependence and is unwise as well. We have all heard of divorces turning nasty when one spouse drains the couple's bank accounts and maxes out credit cards. This same nastiness can also happen when a dating relationship ends. At least in a divorce the judge will sometimes freeze a couple's assets or hold a person responsible to pay back the money. In a dating relationship there is usually little hope of retrieving your money, especially if you shared bank accounts or credit cards. Even in the most amicable dating breakup, this is one area that will sour it quickly.

Another reason not to commingle finances is that there are actually people out there (both male and female) who will enter a dating relationship to gain access to money. There are few worse experiences in life than realizing you've been used or played. It's the perfect setup for depression. You're full of anger at the perpetrator, and you're angry at yourself for allowing it to happen. You also feel embarrassed and foolish in front of family and friends—especially if they tried to warn you and you didn't listen. If someone is pushing you to commingle finances, don't do it. The

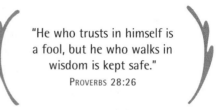

"He who trusts in himself is a fool, but he who walks in wisdom is kept safe."
PROVERBS 28:26

partner with ill intentions will disappear quickly; then you will know his or her motivation for certain.

People can become emotionally overdependent on each other as well. This is often called *codependency*. Pity and guilt are typically used to hold a codependent relationship together. Statements such as "If you leave me, I'd have no reason to live, so I might as well kill myself" are commonly heard in these types of relationships. Guilt is the prime means of motivation—or more accurately, *manipulation*. "You're going to cause me to have a nervous breakdown if you don't make up your mind to marry me or not" was the line one fellow used on his confused girlfriend. In a healthy relationship, that pressure should have cleared up her confusion, causing her to instantly realize that she shouldn't marry him.

Using guilt, pity, or any kind of scare tactic is a form of manipulation and is always self-serving. True love longs to serve the other person first, within appropriate boundaries. Threatening to commit suicide in order to keep someone in a relationship is the lowest form of manipulation there is, but sadly, it is used time and time again.

Should you throw away the umbrella once you're engaged? No.

> "Wounds from a friend can be trusted, but an enemy multiplies kisses."
> PROVERBS 27:6

Did you know that one-third of engagements break up? Unfortunately, too many people confuse engagement with marriage commitment. Is an engagement the same as a lifetime commitment to each other? No. It is a promise of future commitment. Instead of being called boyfriend or girlfriend, you are now called fiancé or fiancée. You are now seeing each other exclusively, planning a marriage ceremony, and making solid plans about the way your future life together might look. However, even though the wedding is being planned, neither person is bound to the other legally or spiritually until the marriage occurs.

We call it the "wedding ceremony," but it is more than just a ceremony—vows are actually taken. It's not like college where once you finish your degree requirements and pay off all those parking tickets, you get a degree whether you attend graduation or not. That is just a ceremony—no vows. The engagement period is the time when you finalize what you already believe to be true: "This is the person I want to spend the rest of my life with." The wedding-planning process is quite telling in terms of what a couple can endure. This is their chance to deal with problems or dissolve the relationship.

Don't let codependency keep you in an unwanted relationship, and don't use manipulation to keep someone else in a relationship with you either. These relationships don't bring fulfillment but, instead, bring resentment. Just as you are the person responsible for your actions, your mate is the one responsible for his actions. In a codependent relationship, your partner actually defines you, because you allow and even enable the other person to dictate your responses.

Don't allow yourself to get caught up in the Abilene Paradox. This term comes from a parable created by management expert Jerry B. Harvey to illustrate how communication breakdowns can lead people to counteract their own preferences. In Harvey's story, four family members in Texas are playing cards on their porch on a hot July afternoon. The father asks if anyone wants to go to Abilene, 60 miles away, for dinner and ice cream. His wife, son, and daughter-in-law all agree to go. The car's air conditioner goes out on the way there, the food is bad, and the service is horrible. The trip back is unpleasant as well. On arriving home, the father says he wished he hadn't gone in the first place. The other family members are angered, saying it was his idea. He defends himself by saying he never really wanted to go but was just throwing out the idea. They were the ones who said yes. It turned out the whole group spent an evening doing something they didn't want to do because no one wanted to risk hurting anyone's feelings.

Marrying a Momma's Boy

Let's talk families again. Remember, families play a large role in making or breaking marriages. When you marry someone, you become part of a new family, your spouse becomes part of yours, and you are beginning your own independent family unit. Family relations should make a marriage stronger, but often this is not the case.

What roles should each of your families play in your relationship? First of all, they should be the supporting cast, not the lead actors. Some parents have a hands-off, distant attitude and have little contact with their newly married child (other than holidays) once the child leaves home. While this is not the ideal supporting role, it rarely causes marital strife. It's the family that stays too much in a young couple's life that ruins marriages—the overly enmeshed families.

You may have laughed at the popular sitcom *Everybody Loves Raymond*, but there are a lot of people in that type of situation and being hurt because of it. Overly intrusive in-laws can ruin a marriage. They may not live right around the corner where they can barge in all day long like Raymond's parents, but today it is easier than ever to intrude in others' lives thanks to cell phones and e-mail.

When family intrusions are not kept in check, the ultimate responsible party is the spouse who did not control his or her parents. Healthy families understand their roles and know when to back off. Dysfunctional families, however, rarely recognize boundaries when it comes to meddling in other family members' business. In truth, mothers-in-law don't have the market cornered on this vice. Fathers, older siblings, and even grandparents are prone to this as well.

Just as a man may be forced to choose between his wife's needs or his mother's wants, a woman may be forced to make a choice between her husband and her family. Older siblings play the role of surrogate parent in some families and may find themselves prying into the marriage relationship as well. To avoid problems, family involvement in your new marriage should be discussed in detail and agreed to many months before the wedding.

As you move closer to a lifelong relationship with the one you love, remember that you cannot give anyone else a drink if your cup is empty. If you see that your own needs are met in a healthy way, your cup will be full, and there will be no room to fill it with empty calories that appear to fill you, but in reality cause starvation. We can all do this if we make unhealthy choices to fill our cups for the moment—in the form of unneeded indulgences or codependent relationships.

Keep your cup full of the things that are healthy for you emotionally so you can build a marriage that will last through difficulties and challenges. A full cup will help your partnership stand strong in both good times and bad.

Reality Check

How have you made healthy decisions regarding whom to date and potentially marry?

How well do you understand your personality? Are you impulsive or compulsive? How has this affected your relationships?

Write It Down

Describe a good dating decision you've made in the past.

Describe a poor dating decision you've made in the past.

What will you do to avoid the misguided decision-making processes described in this chapter?

(9)

Conflict and Communication

Singles say...

...they have made purposeful statements to hurt a partner during an argument.

...they would like better communication skills for all their relationships.

...they would be willing to practice speaking and listening skills, because they believe it will create happier relationships.

Bad relationships have conflict. Good relationships have conflict too. Having more or less conflict does little to determine happiness and satisfaction in a marriage, but *how* you handle it has *everything* to do with it. One of the main ingredients of a successful marriage is the ability to resolve conflict without inflicting pain.

Millions of marriages are miserable. Hang out with one of these miserable couples for any length of time and you will probably discern they lack the ability to resolve conflict in their marriage. It's sad to see two people who are supposed to love and cherish each other get stuck in this situation, especially when it doesn't have to be that way.

These people will make statements such as, "There's no promise that you're supposed to be happy in marriage." They might deny their pain and assure you that their lives are great as they put on forced smiles. All you have to do is watch that couple together and you can see the truth in their eyes. What a tragedy to feel sad around the person who is supposed to be your life partner.

Communication encompasses almost every area of a relationship. Let's focus on one aspect of communication—resolving conflicts. Learning how to efficiently do this will not only make a huge difference in your long-term relationship, but can also be the deciding factor about whether you and your partner want to spend time together or avoid each other.

Much of what we learn about conflict resolution comes from childhood days with our parents. Children raised in chaotic homes where screaming, slamming doors, and ignoring one another were commonplace may see that behavior as normal. A father who screams and yells at his wife when he is angry will most likely produce a son or daughter who screams and yells at his or her spouse when angry. A mother who ignores Dad for weeks following a disagreement will produce a son or daughter who employs the cold shoulder when angered. A child raised in a home where the parents *never* argued in front of the children becomes an adult who thinks any argument in marriage is abnormal.

> "Become a possibilitarian. No matter how dark things seem to be or actually are, raise your sights and see possibilities—always see them for they're always there."
> NORMAN VINCENT PEALE

Amazingly, many couples go into their marriages believing conflict will not be an issue. They point to the fact that their courtships were relatively conflict free. Remember that once a couple begins adding layers to the relationship like family, finances, children, and so on, conflict will build.

What, When, and How

There are three key questions to consider when dealing with conflict. *What* is the conflict actually about? *When* should you work on the conflict? *How* will you resolve it? Let's look at each of these issues—the "what, when, and how"—in detail.

Defining the Issue

Do you always know *what* you are really arguing about? Do you find yourself feeling down even after you feel a problem area has been discussed? Chances are, you might not be dealing with the real problem. Sometimes we have underlying feelings about issues, which we keep buried as we react to the surface layer of the problem. Say your date frequently cancels plans he's made with you when his buddies call. You tell him it upsets you when he does that, and you begin a discussion. You think you have it resolved, but your boyfriend begins to avoid making plans with you if he thinks his friends *might* call, reasoning that he doesn't want to upset you by canceling. He thinks he is doing exactly what you resolved in your discussion, but by now you are really frustrated. Why? Because you have been dealing with the "manners" of the situation. You were right; it was rude and unmannerly of him to behave in that way. In actuality, your core issue was that he was always putting you in second place to his friends.

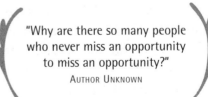

"Why are there so many people who never miss an opportunity to miss an opportunity?"
Author Unknown

This is an example of knowing what effective problem solving is about—knowing what you are in conflict over. This takes practice, so remember it is perfectly fine to revisit issues you have already discussed. As you become more practiced at conflict resolution, you will be able to get to the heart of matters more quickly.

Timing Is Everything

When you work on resolving a conflict is often just as important as knowing *what* the issue is. Remember to use wisdom and discernment before opening your mouth. Ask yourself, *Is this the right time?*

Tact is the art of saying the right thing at the right time. Certain times are inappropriate for discussing disagreements. For instance, while eating dinner with a group of friends, don't take the opportunity to discuss your date's faults. Or discussing an emotionally charged issue is probably not going to go over well after your girlfriend gets reprimanded by her supervisor.

> "Though no one can go back and make a brand new start, anyone can start from now and make a brand new ending."
> CARL BARD

Tactlessness in conflict communication is often the result of selfish motives, with one partner demanding to resolve an issue within his or her own timing without consideration for the other person. Children are often tactless, thinking only about themselves and seeing life solely from their points of view. That may be accepted behavior in a child, but we expect change to occur as manners are mastered and maturity emerges. Ask yourself, *Is my partner ready to hear this now?*

If a couple decides to discuss an issue, but right then is not a good time, the two should simply set a time in the future. A note of caution: In some cases one partner agrees to discuss an issue, then stonewalls for time or doesn't play by the rules. Do not let any issue of concern go longer than one week without discussing it. Set a time, and stick to it.

Doing It Right

How is the third important question in conflict resolution. Remaining calm and sticking to the facts at hand during an argument is paramount to relationship building. You have probably experienced a disagreement that ended up taking two hours of discussion because you rabbit-trailed into multiple other areas. It's best to stick to the issue at hand, because going down rabbit trails will result in not solving the current problem but will open the door for anger and resentment. Keeping calm and reserved will ensure you resolve the problem to everyone's satisfaction.

When appropriate, resolve to lose an argument so you can win a resolution. So how does losing an argument result in a relationship win? It resolves the conflict with the least amount of collateral damage. After all, the goal of disagreements should be to settle the disagreement—not win the argument.

We will look at some positive ways to handle conflict, but first, let's discuss some ways your "vision" affects what conflict looks like.

SEEING THE WORLD THROUGH COLORED GLASSES

The world is full of people who view the world in ways that are not based in truth simply because of their upbringing or personality issues. For example, a person who has been neglected in childhood may often view himself or herself as a victim—of everyone. Every discussion you have with this person ends up with her in tears and "feeling unloved," despite your efforts to do everything right. Additionally, you might spend a good deal of time

> "Destiny is not a matter of chance, it is a matter of choice; it is not a thing to be waited for, it is a thing to be achieved."
> WILLIAM JENNINGS BRYAN

in your relationship attempting to convince this person you aren't cheating, you aren't neglecting him or her, and so forth. In fact, you could be doing everything appropriately, and a counselor would even agree. Understand that negative people are looking at the world through dark-colored glasses. They cannot see the reality of any situation, as they are viewing the world through their past experiences. These experiences act as a filter and affect not only how they view the world, but also how they communicate with others, possibly through accusations, put-downs, withdrawal, and more.

> "What goes into a man's mouth does not make him 'unclean,' but what comes out of his mouth, that is what makes him 'unclean.'"
> MATTHEW 15:11

Following the communication guidelines offered here or in other sources will help but won't be totally effective without education regarding these filters. We all need to know about filters, how they affect us, and how they impact both how we receive and express information. Basically, *message sent* does not necessarily equal *message received,* as filters serve to distort the communication process.

(The following information on filters is based on Christian PREP material developed by Scott M. Stanley, PhD; Daniel W. Tranthen, D.Min., PhD; and Savanna C. McCain, PhD. See www.PREPinc.com.)

Various communication filters can involve the following issues.

1. Inattention: includes hearing and speech problems, environmental noise (TV, kids, computers, etc.), and exhaustion that will prohibit effective communication.

2. Emotional states and reactions: includes emotions such as anger, sadness, or happiness and may be triggered by the present conversation.

3. Beliefs, expectations, and motivations: includes beliefs that affect how things are interpreted. (Example: a person's

raised voice means he outwardly intends to hurt you, or a person's silence means she doesn't care.) This also includes confirmation bias: seeing what you expect to see instead of what is really the truth. It includes how we influence others in our expectations. (Example: a female consistently accuses her date of "cheating." He has never cheated, but after a while, the constant accusations and distrust drive him away, and he ultimately dates someone else behind her back.) It's not wrong to hold on to positive beliefs and expectations if you want to see the good in your dating partner—as long as you aren't in major denial about problems you'd rather ignore. But when you begin negative interpretations that are destructive, you start to expect the worst from your partner.

4. Communication styles: People have different communication styles, including wordy or concise, more or less emotional, and introverted or extroverted. These can lead to irritation or miscommunication. Tolerance of your partner in this area can help alleviate stress.

5. Self-protection: includes covering up your real concerns and feelings out of fear of rejection.

Basically, you should always assume filters are present in every conversation. Have a clear understanding of your own filters first, before you start analyzing anyone else's. As we venture into some great techniques for solving communication problems, consider locating a PREP course in your area. You do not have to be in a relationship to benefit from one of these workshops. They are generally fun and entertaining as well as informative. Contact PREP toll-free at (800) 366-0166 or on the web at PREPinc.com.

COMMUNICATION TECHNIQUES

There are a variety of techniques that contribute to clear communication. Among those we'll explore here are reflective/active listening, using "feeling" or "I" statements, and enlisting written communication.

Reflective/Active Listening

You may have heard of a technique referred to as "reflective listening" or "active listening." This is a simple technique, though it might feel artificial and cheesy when you begin practicing it. The key is to first practice with fun topics and not try to solve problems. After you have practiced this technique for a while, you can begin to incorporate it into problem solving, but it is best to just get the technique down first.

Here are a few ways you can begin to practice this technique and avoid jumping into problem solving prematurely. Try it just like the examples listed, and practice with anyone—friends, relatives, co-workers, or your dates.

Stage-One Exercises

The Drive-Through

(Pretend you're sitting at the drive-through window of a fast-food chain. First, practice communicating the right way.)

> He says: "What would you like to eat?"
>
> She says: "I'd like a foot-long sub with turkey, American cheese, and mustard only. I would also like a large iced tea."
>
> He says: "What I think I hear you saying is you want a foot-long sub with turkey, American cheese, and mustard. You would also like a large iced tea."
>
> She says: "Yes, thank you, that's correct."

(Next, consider the wrong type of communication.)

He says: "What would you like to eat?"

She says: "I'd like a foot-long sub with turkey, American cheese, and mustard only. I would also like a large iced tea."

He says: "For five cents more you could also get a bag of chips. Don't you want me to get you a bag?"

(Remember, at this stage you are only to practice the technique. You can add probing questions later. Practice the simple technique listed first and get it down solidly before you begin asking questions and clarifying.)

The Fantasy Vacation
(First, try this dialogue, demonstrating the right way.)

He says: "I would love to go to Florida so I could lounge on the beach and get away from phones and people demanding my time."

She says: "What I think you're telling me is you want to go to Florida to lounge on the beach and escape phone calls and people demanding your time."

He says: "Yes, thanks, that's right."

(Next, consider the wrong way to communicate.)

He says: "I would love to go to Florida so I could lounge on the beach and get away from phones and people demanding my time."

She says: "Wouldn't you rather go out of the country where your cell phone can't be accessed?"

(Okay, by now you get the idea. After you have mastered this, you can begin to insert some clarification questions.)

Stage-Two Exercises

The Drive-Through

(Pretend you are sitting at the drive-through window of a fast-food chain. First, practice the dialogue, demonstrating the right way.)

He says: "What would you like to eat?"

She says: "I'd like a foot-long sub with turkey, American cheese, and mustard only. I would also like a large iced tea."

He says: "What I think I hear you saying is you want a foot-long sub with turkey, American cheese, and mustard. You would also like a large iced tea."

She says: "Yes, thank you, that's correct."

He says: "Let me clarify two things: First, would you like anything for your tea such as lemon or sugar? Second, for five cents more you could get a bag of chips. Would you like one?"

She says: "Yes, thanks for asking. I would like lemon only with my tea, and I would like a bag of tortilla chips."

He says: "Okay, what I hear you saying is you want a foot-long sub with turkey, American cheese, and mustard. You would also like a large iced tea with lemon, and a bag of tortilla chips."

She says: "Yes, thanks, that's exactly what I want."

(Next, consider the wrong type of communication.)

He says: "What would you like to eat?"

She says: "I'd like a foot-long sub with turkey, American cheese, and mustard only. I would also like a large iced tea."

He says: "For five cents more you could also get a bag of chips."

She says: "But I'm not hungry for chips. I don't think I could eat them."

He says: "It just seems silly not to get it at that price."

(As you can imagine, things go downhill quickly at this point.)

The Fantasy Vacation
(Try this exercise the right way first.)

He says: "I would love to go to Florida so I could lounge on the beach and get away from phones and people demanding my time."

She says: "What I think you're telling me is you want to go to Florida to lounge on the beach and escape phone calls and people demanding your time."

He says: "Yes, thanks, that's right."

She says: "Are you just totally wanting to relax on the beach or would you also like to spend some time sightseeing?"

He says: "That's a great question. I would like to spend the first half of each day lounging, and then spend evenings sightseeing and going out to dinner."

She says: "I think you are saying that you want to relax on the beach, but spend the evening going out."

He says: "Yes, that's correct."

She says: "Tell me what time you consider 'evening.'"

He says: "Good thought. I would like to be cleaned up and leave the hotel by five o'clock nightly."

She says: "What you're saying is that you would like to go to Florida, lounge on the beach, and get away from people and phones. You would also like to be cleaned up and leave the hotel by five o'clock nightly to go to dinner and do some sightseeing."

He says: "Yes, thanks for helping me clarify; that's correct."

(Next, consider the wrong type of communication.)

He says:	"I would love to go to Florida so I could lounge on the beach and get away from phones and people demanding my time."
She says:	"Wouldn't you rather go out of the country where your cell phone can't be accessed? By the way, that sounds boring if you're just going to lounge on the beach. If you're going that far and spending that much money, don't you want to do anything else that might be fun while you are there?"

Feelings and "I" Statements

When you give someone an idea about how a problem makes you feel, you stand a better chance of achieving a positive resolution. Performing this technique the right way also allows the other person *not* to be put on the defensive, which blocks effective communication.

Let's look at how to effectively use this technique, also incorporating reflective listening and effectively probing into the statements your partner is making. You will also see a solution offered at the end of the conversation.

He says:	"I feel angry when you wait until the last minute to ask me to fill your tank up with gas."
She says:	"You feel angry when I wait until the last minute to ask you to fill my tank up with gas."
He says:	"Yes, that's correct."
She says:	"What exactly causes you to be angry when I wait until the last minute?"
He says:	"We both work the eleven P.M. shift. I feel angry if I happen to leave for work before you some evening

and you haven't asked me to fill your tank, because you might have to stop by yourself at night and get gas. I feel it's unsafe for you to do that, and I worry about you. If anything ever happened to you, I don't know what I would do."

She says: "So you become angry because I am putting myself in an unsafe situation, and you worry about me."

He says: "Yes, that's correct. May I also say something else?"

She says: "Yes, go ahead."

He says: "I really need to trust that you will always let me know when you're low on gas. You've failed to do this several times, and I end up worrying about you when I get to work. Since I work with patients, I need to know 100 percent of the time that you are safe. That is my priority, along with making sure I don't make a mistake with a patient because I am worrying about you gassing up at night by yourself."

She says: "Okay, so in addition to your worrying about me, you also want to know that you can trust me, and that will help ensure you don't make a mistake with a patient because you are worrying about me."

He says: "Yes, you totally understand."

She says: "That is so sweet. I never knew you felt that way, and it helps me know why you seem to get frustrated. Thank you for caring about me and your patients. May I suggest another idea?"

He says: "That would be great, go ahead."

She says: "Now that I know how you feel, I promise never to wait until the last minute to get gas. But why don't we make a deal? We both get up early each afternoon. Let's agree to get up for the day, eat lunch, and then go check both cars immediately after lunch. This will

> allow both of us to feel assured that if either of us needs gas, we can take care of it at that time. It will become a habit."
>
> He says:　　"So you want to get up for the day, eat lunch, and check both cars immediately after lunch. We'll go together to fill up the tanks if necessary."
>
> She says:　"Yes, that's exactly what I'd like to do."
>
> He says:　　"I think that's a great idea. Let's start today."

As you can see, the couple has obviously done this enough that they don't have to stick strictly to the format as earlier described. But you can see how they stick to the intent of the techniques, and it provides a viable solution, as well as increasing positive feelings and respect for each other.

The Power of the Pen

Sometimes when a conflict appears, it is best to write things down prior to discussion. This is a good technique for those who are less able to verbalize or those people who always intend to say the right thing but find that it comes out wrong in the moment. This would also be a good technique for people who have not yet totally overcome their filters, making spoken communication less effective. They never quite "hear" anything or "express" anything as it really is intended.

Here's how to try this technique.

- Write down the conflict or problem area.
- List three ways *you* contribute to the problem. (You will be surprised how this defuses anger and resentment and opens the door to working together.)
- List three options for resolution.
- Have your partner do the same thing.

- Talk over your list first, with no judgment or discussion.
- Next, have your partner talk about his or her list, with no judgment or discussion.
- Ask your partner which of the three options on your list he or she would like to try.
- Your partner should tell you his choice.
- Select one solution on your partner's list to try. (Obviously, if you both have come up with one or more solutions that are the same, choose one of those.) Flip a coin to see which one you will do first. Begin the following day, and try the "winning" solution for a week.
- After a week, discuss how it went. If the issue is settled, move on.
- If it is not settled, try the other solution for one week. After that week, discuss again.

By that point, if the solution is not working, you can both redo your lists. You'll be surprised at how you might actually come up with the same solution ideas the next time around.

~

Reality Check

Whether you are single or in a relationship, find a PREP or CPREP course in your area and attend it.

If you are in a serious dating relationship, take the PREP course, and also find a counselor who is trained in the Prepare/Enrich program. The PREP course begins with an online assessment of many aspects of your relationship: your individual personalities, your "couple" personality, your families of origin, and various components of your relationship such as finances, marital expectations, spirituality, communication, conflict resolution, friends and family influences, and so on. You can go online to Prepare-Enrich and find a counselor in your area (www.prepare-enrich.com).

Read at least one book about relationships from one of the following authors:
- Les and Leslie Parrot
- Gary Chapman
- Gary Smalley
- Henry Cloud
- John Townsend
- Scott Stanley

Write It Down and Discuss

Consider these areas highlighted by the Prepare-Enrich inventories for premarital and married couples. Write down your feelings about each issue, and if you are in a relationship, consider these areas as a team. If you are not currently in a relationship, bounce your ideas and expectations off family and friends—at least those whom you trust for honest feedback.

Marriage Expectations: How do you define being a good husband or wife? What do you expect of yourself as a spouse? What do you expect of your intended as a spouse? What will your day-to-day life be like? What is your mission for life, and how does that fit in to the mission of your potential marriage?

Personality Issues: What personality issues of your own do you believe could be potentially problematic for others in relationship with you? What personality issues of others cause you irritation? Show your answers to your friends and family, and ask them for feedback.

Communication: Do you communicate well? If not, what are your weaknesses, and how can you strengthen them? If possible, get feedback from your partner and as many close friends and family members as you can.

Conflict Resolution: Are you as skilled as you want to be with conflict resolution? Practice the techniques in this book. Write down names of people with whom you have difficulty communicating, and list the reasons why. What can you do to improve this situation on your end?

Financial Management: Do you have a budget and stick to it? Where do you see yourself financially in 5, 10, and 20 years? How are you going to get there? If you are in a relationship, how will that fit in? Does your future spouse agree with most of your ideas in this category?

Friends and Family: Do you get along with your family? Do you get along with your partner's friends and family? Do they feel they get along with you? How do you see those relationships fitting in to your life as a married person? What percentage of your time and energy will go into those relationships once you're married?

Children and Parenting: How many children do you want? How long after you're married will you begin having children? How does this fit in to your financial career plan? What kinds of ideas do you have about parenting? Does your partner agree? How similar or different are your families of origin, and what challenges relate to incorporating both families' values into your own household?

Leisure Activities: What do you like to do for leisure activities? How much time will be devoted to this once you're married? Do you feel the need for your partner to participate in these activities? How much? What leisure activities can you see yourself participating in on your own, and what activities can you do with your partner?

Sexual Expectations: Sexual expectations have to do with much more than sexual activity. This category also has to do with intimacy. Even if you have taken a purity vow, you still must discuss this category. It is important you understand the intimacy issues and ideas about sex that you both bring into the relationship. How do you feel about sexual issues? Are they to be openly discussed, or are they taboo? Do you discuss sexual issues with friends and family, or do you intend to keep that private between the two of you? Are you comfortable with the sexual history of the other person, and will you resolve those issues prior to marriage?

Role Relationship: How do you feel about who does what? Do you feel that the woman should stay home while the man makes a living? Is it suitable for the woman to manage the finances if that is her talent? Is it all right for the woman to mow the lawn or the man to do the laundry? These are issues related to the roles you have in your relationship. The answers to these questions are not what's important; the important part is *do you agree with your partner about these issues?*

Spiritual Beliefs: Spiritual beliefs are extremely important in a marital relationship. What are your ideas about how spiritual or religious beliefs and practices will affect your relationship? How often will you attend services, if at all? Will you incorporate spiritual activities in your daily life and relationship? How will you incorporate this aspect once you have children?

If you can begin to answer these questions on your own, as well as with your future spouse, you will have a greater understanding of where you both stand regarding your upcoming marital relationship. If you do these exercises right, you should have few surprises to handle once you become husband and wife.

(10)

Making the Most of Every Stage

Singles say…

> …they believe they will find a partner who is "right" for them.
>
> …they sometimes question if they know how to recognize that person due to past mistakes.
>
> …they want to structure relationships in the future to minimize problems down the road.

If you follow every commandment in this chapter, you'll begin to see positive changes in your personal life, your dating life, your engagement life, and all your relationships. If there are components listed that you cannot embrace, consider consulting a counselor to find out why. These principles are intended to help you experience success in your relationships, and they start with *your* core. You are worthy of being loved and adored, so before you decide on the love of your life, do the following:

TEN COMMANDMENTS OF DATING

1. *Believe in* and *be true* to yourself. Ensure you are a self-aware person of growth in all areas of your life, and then truly believe in your-

self. Refine yourself to be the best you can be, for the purpose you were intended. Know yourself intimately. Hope and believe the best about yourself and the people in your life, but make sure to represent who you *truly* are in terms of both strengths and growth areas, and expect that from the other person as well.

2. You have made your wish list; now stick with it. Understand the principle of delayed gratification by thinking about the rest of your life instead of just today. It is better to invest in wise, thoughtful choices *now* that will pay off a hundredfold in the long run.

3. Look at the dates you have attracted thus far, and decide if you need to change your plan to get new results. The plan might include self-improvement, relationship classes, or simply figuring out where to find great dates. Don't keep looking for dates at your friend's favorite dance club if you're looking for the intellectual, quiet type. Understand timing within your plan. If you're not completely ready, wait until you are. Make good habits and repetition part of your plan, and don't give up if it takes time. You might occasionally need to make slight changes to the plan, but stay with strategies that make the best sense, such as finding that quiet intellectual type at chamber of commerce meetings or business conferences. (Just brush up on your business sense *before* you go so you can make great small talk.)

> "Associate yourself with men of good quality if you esteem your own reputation; for 'tis better to be alone than in bad company."
> GEORGE WASHINGTON

4. Do what it takes to get what you want. Stop old habits, and make new ones to produce a new result. If you like athletes, go where the athletes are. If you like musicians, go where the musicians are. If you attract the wrong type of musicians and athletes, then go where the right ones are. If you want a person who shares your faith, go to the church where you can find that person, instead of a bar where you probably won't.

5. Get your life organized. Plan a schedule and stick to it as much as possible. You won't meet the right dates for you if you allow yourself to be pulled in everyone else's direction. You can participate in a lot of fun or worthwhile activities, but will they get you what you want? Do you want to lose 10 pounds so

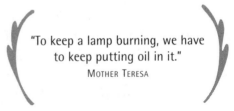

"To keep a lamp burning, we have to keep putting oil in it."
MOTHER TERESA

you feel good about yourself when you meet new people? Then don't get dragged to the buffet every night by your friends if you have made a plan to exercise after work.

6. Rest! Fifteen minutes of rest each day—praying, relaxing, meditating—will help you stay focused and calm. In addition, spend four hours, once a week, relaxing, making plans for your upcoming week, and doing something just for you. Taking time to meet your own needs will help you resist looking to others to meet them for you.

7. Go where you are appreciated and don't have to "prove yourself." Don't spend one minute attempting to convince anyone of your assets, and don't spend time listening to people who put you down—particularly if their words are unsolicited. Your confidence in yourself must be untainted if you are going to attract the right person. Many people find that when they are down, they attract relationships that not only cause pain in the end, but don't last.

8. Keep the boundaries you set in your plan, and gather information through the various stages of disclosure before making any commitments. Spend appropriate time with potential dates, and ask questions. Do not compromise. If your date tries to force you into moving too quickly, do not be swayed. You know what's right for you, and compromising now sets you up to compromise later.

9. Remember that every date does not have to end in a relationship; every connection may lead you to other connections. Keep

your boundaries clear and proceed with caution. As you act with honesty and integrity, you will keep the friendships you acquire through the dating process, even if you don't connect romantically. One date does not obligate you to anyone. Until you and your date agree to date exclusively, you are both free to spend time with other people. Just make sure there is an understanding here or one of you may be hurt.

10. Keep growing—even before you begin dating great people. Read books, attend workshops, or seek counseling. The more information you obtain, the more you will be able to focus your search in detail and hopefully with more success. This approach will help you personally and in all your relationships.

THE TEN COMMANDMENTS OF ENGAGEMENT

Scientists say that every seven years the human body completely renews itself. In other words, seven years from now the trillions of cells that make up your body today will have been replaced by new ones, and your body will look different. This happens as a gradual process. Relationships need renewing too. People change. This is also a gradual process.

The good-looking guy with the full head of black wavy hair will look different in 50 years. He will also act differently, but then again, so will you. Going water skiing at the lake or the way your jeans make your backside look will probably not be important to you in 50 years. Aspects of life that you hardly give a second thought to now, such as how your bowels are working, will likely have more meaning to you as you reach your golden anniversary.

How do two people in a relationship for life keep these changes from diminishing their love and enjoyment of each other? By sticking to the alphabet: Consider the following ABC's of a fulfilling marriage as your Ten Commandments of Engagement. They should be employed during the engagement period and continued through your married life. Wedding planning is important, but the most important planning you will do is *relationship* planning. This is where you take everything you have learned and start applying it in the final stages of dating—before you walk down the aisle.

Here are ten relationship-planning steps that will help you stay happy and fulfilled in your rela-

> "To change and to change for the better are two different things."
> GERMAN PROVERB

tionship during the years to come. Remember, your goal is "till death do us part," and hopefully that will be a long time. Do your best to make it a wonderful journey.

Annual Executive Retreat

Many successful corporations have annual retreats where the leaders take time off and travel to a secluded destination. The purpose is discussion and analysis of annual organizational performance as well as strategy for the future. Executives will tell you this is imperative for future company strength, cohesiveness, growth, productivity, morale, and teamwork. Couples, too, should have their own executive retreat.

Begin miniretreats before your wedding. Six months prior to your wedding, sit down on an evening where you have one to four hours to set up a life plan. It can be as simple or complicated as you want to make it. And if you really want to make this evening productive, consider using a therapist or counselor specializing in marriage issues.

Discuss the vital issues offered in the chapter 9 Write It Down and Discuss section. Make this experience fun! Do not use this time to bicker and create dissension. Write down your plans as if creating a business proposal.

Following that first retreat, set aside an evening each week to revisit these topics. It doesn't need to be a long meeting—usually 15 minutes to an hour will suffice. These sessions are great tools to defuse issues before they grow into conflict and anger. You should table heated debates that arise until the weekly meeting, unless they need to be managed immediately. This weekly meeting will keep your lines of communication open and will keep you both in problem-solving mode and away from the destructive habit of sweeping issues under the rug.

> "If a man has recently married, he must not be sent to war or have any other duty laid on him." (Application: Take time to nourish the relationship!)
> DEUTERONOMY 24:5

Married couples should continue this practice and add an annual retreat, the first of which should be scheduled at least one month after the first anniversary. This doesn't have to be an expensive trip to the Bahamas but could consist of spending the weekend at a local hotel. Going somewhere outside the home will decrease distractions. Leaving the kids, dog, laundry, and chores behind will help you stay on task.

Benefits of Continued Practice

Professional athletes generally start their yearly season with a training camp. They start practicing weeks before their first game and continue practicing between games all season long. They know practicing will help them succeed as a team. Waiting until the season began before starting to practice would put the team at a huge disadvantage. Likewise in marriage, it doesn't make much sense to wait until you're married to start practicing for success. The more practice you have in dealing with problems, the more efficiently you'll handle them.

You can even practice on your own before you meet your mate. Here are some ideas.

- Read a book on relationships.
- Read a book on communication skills.
- Select a weekly communication skill to work on with friends or coworkers.
- Practice your listening skills.

Celebrate Good Times

Birthdays and anniversaries are important, but it's also important to celebrate other events: a new job, a promotion, or finally cleaning out all those closets. These are constant reminders that we have many things for which to be grateful. A celebration might be going out to dinner or just going out for a special dessert after dinner. It could be going to the lake, renting a movie, or having a picnic—things that don't cost a lot of money but create memories. Keeping a grateful, thankful state of mind becomes a habit that will flow to every area of your life and marriage.

Celebrating each other should be a daily activity. Your relationship will benefit if you make a constant effort each day to affirm your partner about something you appreciate in him or her. It could be as simple as "I love your eyes," or "thank you for always taking the trash out." One sweet statement can make you feel like you are celebrating a good time when you never even left your kitchen.

Deepen Your Love

In our busy world of jobs, hectic schedules, and poor sleep habits we sometimes become cranky and tired. When we do, it can be difficult to view our partners and relationships in a positive light. It's no excuse, but it does happen. So how do you deepen your love in times like these? Think about your mate's character—the wonderful aspects. Take a few minutes each day to ruminate on those things. Think about his or her physical characteristics that you absolutely love. Send your mate a voice message or e-mail that says, "Thanks for loving me," or "You are so thoughtful."

Determine to do something for your partner that he or she would love—whether you love it or not. Nothing will deepen your love more than carving out a small amount of time for meeting each other's needs.

Emulate the Experts

Marriage experts do not necessarily have to author books and videos, but they need to be people with stable successful marriages who have at least a few decades under their belts. Finding a married couple to mentor you is a wise move. It's okay to find a couple with faults. The key is to not idolize or copy the couple, but to evaluate their faults, understand how they overcame obstacles, and then begin creating your own map of marriage success. You might not have the same problems or even want to handle issues in the same ways they have. Rather, the creative thoughts and ideas you obtain from others will inspire you, give you hope, and stimulate you to keep moving forward for your couple success.

First Things First

Stephen Covey, author of *The 7 Habits of Highly Effective People*, points out that at the end of the day, you might have accomplished many wonderful things, but did you accomplish your A priority? Are you good at keeping first things first, or do you sacrifice the most important priorities of your life at the whim of everything and everyone that comes your way?

You may be multitalented and have a servant's heart. If that is the case, you *will* be constantly asked to do many things that take time away from the primary commitments in your life. While you may continue to serve others, realize that during certain times of life you need to say no more often, because saying yes might take you away from your A priority.

Your first priority should be God. Following the tenets of your faith will give you a strong base on which to build all your interpersonal relationships. This is key to staying grounded for the good of all areas and relationships in your life.

> "A wife of noble character is her husband's crown, but a disgraceful wife is like decay in his bones."
> PROVERBS 12:4

If you decide to marry, the second priority is your commitment to the marriage relationship. That doesn't mean you have to stay home from work to coddle your spouse. What it does mean is leaving your father and mother (and friends in some cases) and being united to your spouse. No, don't ditch the family and friends, but remember that you took vows about the marriage, which makes it your second-place commitment, after God. When children arrive, they become part of your own family priority. Family of origin, friends, career, and leisure time are all important in life, but they come after the marriage and family relationship in priority. Be sure to discuss as a couple how your priorities will be arranged.

Give to Others

There are people in the world who have never lifted a finger to help another person—hard to believe, but true. Continue to be a giver in whatever way you are called to give. You might participate in dog-sitting, worldwide missions, helping the elderly, baby-sitting for frazzled moms, fixing cars, making baby scrapbooks for new moms, or taking your coworker for bagels and coffee. Every person is called to give to the world in some way, so do it. Do what you feel called to do, and don't let anyone minimize your way of serving. Getting outside of yourself on a regular basis will help you keep a healthy perspective on life.

Giving to others actually strengthens all your other relationships. It also keeps you from focusing on how traumatic it was that the tile guy was 15 minutes late yesterday for that repair job. When you're aware of others' needs, you begin to see how blessed your life is, and you're able to let go of the small stuff that just doesn't matter.

Happiness Happens

Happiness happens all the time, but do you see it? You'll find wonderful things happening around you when you look for them. An unhappy man thinks angrily, *My paycheck is short this week!* A grateful, happy man thinks, *My paycheck is short, but at least I have one. I'll now get an opportunity to network with my boss to get this fixed.*

Now, of course, happy people don't go around thinking this way *all* the time. We all get frustrated. You can get annoyed at the guy who cuts you off in traffic and stew all day about it, or you can think, *I'm glad I left home early and don't have to rush like that guy.* Little tricks that help you reframe frustrating situations will help you stay calm, look at life with a sense of humor, and increase your joy and gratitude. This happens because you are no longer letting your emotions control you. I'm not suggesting you ignore problems. Do address them head-on. Just address them in a positive way that results in a successful, win-win outcome.

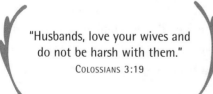

"Husbands, love your wives and do not be harsh with them."
COLOSSIANS 3:19

Happiness happens more abundantly to those who perceive it. Internal happiness will affect your relationships and every other aspect of your life just as unhappiness and resentment will infect every area of your life.

Ignore the Busybodies

How do meddling people affect your relationship? They try to derail it in their own special way, sometimes on purpose and sometimes just simply because they're "challenged." Do not share the details of your relationship with anyone who will give you an unsolicited opinion. Your relationship is none of their business. Also be wise about who you consult when you do want an opinion. The rule of thumb is this: Go to a counselor or unbiased person when you want relationship advice. Asking for advice automatically puts your personal information in play for others. As amazing as your parents, siblings, or best friend might be, you would be surprised at how, over time, this could come back to bite you and your spouse. Again, however, if everyone you know is telling you the relationship you are in is not positive, seek counseling immediately. This goes beyond the busybody who is attempting to be nosey.

Jump Wisely!

Diving-board injuries don't usually result from lack of skill, talent, or intelligence, but from a lack of concentration, caution, and safety. Carelessness and the resulting injuries have prompted some pool owners to remove the diving boards, ruining fun for others.

Marriage involves risk, just like jumping off a diving board does. There's no guarantee you will avoid injury. Many people who have been injured in bad relationships will be the first to tell you they were just like the overzealous kid at the swimming pool—lack of caution or concentration caused the injury. In retrospect they admit that seeing the warning signs during the dating period but not giving them full attention resulted in hurt. Many of these people swear off relationships for good, never realizing it was *their* own lack of caution that resulted in heartache, not the other person or the institution of the relationship. If you overlook something in your dating period that causes injury, just deal with it without judgment. If you deal with it effectively, your hurts will heal, and you will be stronger. You and your eventual mate will continue to make mistakes all your lives; accept them, deal with them, learn from them, and make positive changes.

SOME FINAL THOUGHTS

Relationship success consists of three main ingredients:
Finding the right person for *you*
Understanding what the marriage commitment means
Working smarter, not harder, by:
- Remembering your partner's assets, thinking about the wonderful life and times together that you share, and letting each other know those things every day
- Keeping honest communication lines open and never breaking trust
- Committing to calmly resolve issues, not be a winner

Remember that together, you *will* be creating exactly the kind of relationship you desire, so you might as well make it a good one.

Reality Check

What are three things you will do *differently* to work smarter, not harder, in your relationship?

Write It Down

After you write this, repeat it to yourself on an ongoing basis.

I was created for a purpose full of life, joy, and peace.

I choose to attract the kind of relationships that further my purpose.

I choose the thoughts and attitudes that attract all the good relationships in my life.

I accept that I do not have power over everything that comes my way.

I accept the power to control my perception of, and response to, the events of life.

I accept that my perceptions and responses are catalysts for life's future successes or failures.

I choose to accept my life's purpose with joy and peace.

Here's to happy dating and much happiness for your future.

FOCUS ON THE FAMILY®

Welcome to the family!

Whether you purchased this book, borrowed it, or received it as a gift, we're glad you're reading it. It's just one of the many helpful, encouraging, and biblically based resources produced by Focus on the Family for people in all stages of life.

Focus began in 1977 with the vision of one man, Dr. James Dobson, a licensed psychologist and author of numerous best-selling books on marriage, parenting, and family. Alarmed by the societal, political, and economic pressures that were threatening the existence of the American family, Dr. Dobson founded Focus on the Family with one employee and a once-a-week radio broadcast aired on 36 stations.

Now an international organization reaching millions of people daily, Focus on the Family is dedicated to preserving values and strengthening and encouraging families through the life-changing message of Jesus Christ.

Focus on the Family Magazines

These faith-building, character-developing publications address the interests, issues, concerns, and challenges faced by every member of your family from preschool through the senior years.

| Focus on the Family **Citizen®** U.S. news issues | Focus on the Family **Clubhouse Jr.™** Ages 4 to 8 | Focus on the Family **Clubhouse™** Ages 8 to 12 | **Breakaway®** Teen guys | **Brio®** Teen girls 12 to 16 | **Brio & Beyond®** Teen girls 16 to 19 | **Plugged In®** Reviews movies, music, TV |

FOR MORE INFORMATION

Online:
Log on to www.family.org
In Canada, log on to www.focusonthefamily.ca

Phone:
Call toll free: (800) A-FAMILY (232-6459)
In Canada, call toll free: (800) 661-9800

Make the most of your relationships with resources from Focus on the Family®!

From dating and engagement to the wedding and beyond, we're here to help your marriage thrive.

First Comes Love, Then What?
Myths about finding Mr. or Mrs. Right are held to be true by too many men and women searching for that one-in-a-million match. It's time for a reality check. Filled with real-life examples and solid principles, this book will help both men and women learn to use their heads before losing their hearts.
Paperback F00727B

Countdown for Couples
Research and common sense indicate that engaged couples will have stronger, more successful marriages if they participate in premarital counseling. Yet with all the planning that goes into a wedding, this important preparation can often be overlooked. *Countdown for Couples* delivers insight in an easy-to-use format and tackles important questions such as: *Are you ready for a lifelong commitment? What should you expect?* And more!
Paperback F00863B

The Savvy Bride's Answer Guide
Your maid of honor might not tell you, but the price of your wedding dress isn't the only thing that may shock you about wedded bliss. During the first year of marriage, you're likely to face all kinds of surprises—from your in-laws' strange traditions to your groom's annoying tendencies. This friendly resource will smooth the road whether you've been engaged for 10 minutes or married for 10 months.
Paperback F00857B

The Smart Groom's Answer Guide
Launching your lifetime love? Getting biblical answers is the smart thing to do! This book provides down-to-earth advice from a team of professional Focus on the Family counselors. You'll get the real story on questions like *What does it mean to be a husband? Why does she want to talk all the time?* And more! Ask now—or forever hold your peace!
Paperback F00856B

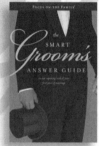

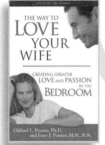